Media and Development

The Road Ahead

Media and Development

The Road Ahead

By

Madhuri Madhok
Assistant Professor,
Journalism and Mass Communication,
Indian Institute of Mass Communication (IIMC), New Delhi

New Century Publications
New Delhi, India

NEW CENTURY PUBLICATIONS
4800 / 24, Bharat Ram Road,
Ansari Road, Daryaganj,
New Delhi - 110 002 (India)

Tel.: 011-2324 7798, 4358 7398, 4101 7798
E-mail: indiatax@vsnl.com • info@newcenturypublications.com
www.newcenturypublications.com

Editorial office:
LG – 7, Aakarshan Bhawan,
4754-57/23, Ansari Road, Daryaganj,
New Delhi – 110 002

Tel.: 011-4356 0919

First Published: **2018**

ISBN: **978-81-7708-464-1**

Published by New Century Publications and printed at Milan Enterprises, New Delhi.

Designs: Patch Creative Unit, New Delhi.

PRINTED IN INDIA

Dedicated to My Respected Father

Professor Balraj Madhokji

A Great Visionary, Ideologue, Statesman, Thinker and Writer
A True Karma Yogi, Gyan Yogi and Dhyan Yogi

About the Book

Development aims at bringing about qualitative changes leading to an upward movement of the entire social system. It is measured in terms of improvement in the lives of the people and strengthening of the individual's and thereby a nation's capacity to deal with the rest of the world. Development is, therefore, interlinked with the entire social, political and cultural fabric of a society.

This comprehensive approach to human development takes care of all other approaches such as the human resources approach; the basic needs approach and the human welfare approach. The slogan *Sabka Saath, Sabka Vikas* aptly sums up the basic principles of this development model which aims at *Sarve Bhavantu Sukhinah,* i.e. let all be prosperous and happy.

Both demographic explosion and terrorism pose a serious threat to development. Unchecked population not only slows down the pace of development but also accentuates the ecological crisis thereby preventing the benefits of development from reaching one and all. Terrorism reduces the scope, the magnitude and beneficial impact of development everywhere.

This book is an incisive study of the dynamics of development. It combines both theoretical underpinnings and practical insights to enlighten the reader about various challenges on the path to development. Written by a journalist and a media academic, it is invaluable—to both media practitioners and students—in understanding the fine nuances of the current development discourse.

About the Author

Dr. Madhuri Madhok is a veteran journalist and media academic. She has been associated as Assistant Professor, Journalism and Mass Communication, Indian Institute of Mass Communication (IIMC), New Delhi. She has been a visiting faculty at the University of Delhi and a media counsellor of Indira Gandhi National Open University (IGNOU).

She started writing for the print media from her college days and covered the Punjab crisis in the mid-1980s while pursuing her Masters in English from the University of Delhi. She joined the Press Trust of India (PTI)—India's premier news agency—in 1986, and covered Parliament and Central Ministries including Ministry of Energy and Environment as well as various assembly and general elections.

Her incisive news features on India's bilateral relations with other countries fetched her media fellowship to Israel in 1997. She also served as the editor-in-charge of the weekly news bulletin *The Economic News from India,* published by the PTI for the Ministry of External Affairs. Her published books include: *Portraits of Patriots; News Media in India: The Impact of Globalization; News Agency Journalism;* and *News and Social Media: Redefining Journalism.*

New Delhi-based Dr. Madhok has been a resource person for various communication courses organized by IIMC for the officers of Indian Armed Forces. She has organized workshops on media and related issues for the students of journalism and media practitioners alike. She has also participated in various national and international seminars and conferences organized by the UNESCO, UNDP, FICCI and CII. She is currently engaged in media research and regularly writes on various national and international issues in mainstream print and online media including *The Sunday Guardian.*

Contents

Preface

Development is the key to progress. It is measured in terms of improvement in the lives of the people and strengthening of the individual's and thereby a nation's capacity to deal with the rest of the world. Development is, therefore, interlinked with the entire social, political and cultural fabric of the society. It aims at bringing about qualitative changes leading to an upward movement of the entire social system.

Development is a chain process. If one region develops, the adjoining region also develops. It gives impetus to development in all the regions that are economically connected with the adjoining region. Similarly, lack of development in one region promotes underdevelopment or slows down the pace of development in the adjoining region as well. This should be kept in mind during developmental planning.

Both demographic explosion and terrorism pose a serious threat to development. The vicious nexus between poverty and uncontrolled population is a huge obstacle in the way of achieving development objectives. Unchecked population not only slows down the pace of development but also accentuates the ecological crisis thereby preventing the benefits of development from reaching one and all.

Terrorism reduces the scope, the magnitude and beneficial impact of development everywhere. It not only derails development but also destroys the agents of change. People who are involved in bringing about development along with infrastructure and other wherewithal are lost due to terrorist activities. This creates terror in the minds of those people who are going to benefit most from the development. Terrorism prevents participation, adds to the cost of development and minimizes the human and material benefits accruing from it.

Since development, like freedom and sovereignty, is indivisible, its fruits and benefits can be shared, but its progress cannot be allowed to get thwarted. And, given the enormous power and reach of the media— both new as well as traditional—

it is incumbent upon their practitioners and students alike to have a clear understanding of the dynamics of development and related issues. It is in this context that the study of development journalism holds such a special place in media academics.

This book has been written to enlighten the discerning readers about the prospects and challenges in the path to development. It encompasses a detailed study of issues and concerns in the current discourse on development.

I humbly dedicate this book to my respected father Professor Balraj Madhok for his selfless service to the nation. As co-founder of Bhartiya Jan Sangh in 1951, he wrote its manifesto where he gave the concept of *Jankalyanwad*, i.e. welfare for all through popular participation as against state control in the name of socialism or *samajwad*. He also enunciated the idea of India in his iconic book *Indianisation* where he gave the clarion call for India First.

Madhuri Madhok

Introduction

Development is a journey, not a destination. It encompasses all aspects and facets of human life from birth to death. It includes basic material needs like food, clothing and shelter to higher ones such as social, mental, intellectual, emotional and spiritual aspirations culminating in man's eternal quest for self-actualization through optimization of his full potential as the Almighty's supreme creation on mother earth.

Development is a process. It is not an event or a happening to be reported as breaking news. As a long drawn process, it may stretch over days, months, years, decades and even centuries. However, the success of a developmental initiative largely depends on the will of the nation and sincerity of its political leadership to see it through amidst all adversity. After all, what cuts deep in politics cuts deep all around.

Development is the key to success. It ensures growth and prosperity for any nation. The real objective of development, according to the United Nations Development Programme (UNDP), is to increase people's developmental choices to make development more democratic and participatory. These choices should include access to income and employment opportunities, education and health, and a clean and safe physical environment. However, enhancing the choices of one individual, or one section of society, should not restrict the choices of another. This calls for equity in human relationships. This can be done by building human capabilities and ensuring basic freedoms to achieve their dreams and aspirations in life by realizing their full potential.

Development is democratic. It provides equal opportunity to each and every individual to participate freely and fearlessly in all community decisions and to enjoy social, economic and political freedoms responsibly. This sentiment is expressed in the Preamble to the Indian Constitution adopted on November 26, 1949. Committed to the provision of a just and equitable social order in which equality of status and opportunity is assured to all and not only to a few, the Preamble states: "As a SOVEREIGN,

SOCIALIST, SECULAR AND DEMOCRATIC REPUBLIC, India is committed to secure to all its citizens social, economic and political JUSTICE; LIBERTY of thought, expression, belief, faith and worship; EQUALITY of status, and of opportunity, and to promote to them all, FRATERNITY assuring the dignity of the individual and the unity and integrity of the Nation".

Development is participatory. It allows for private initiative and broad-based people's involvement at all levels—individual, local, national, international—and distributed well and benefiting all people. According to social scientist Paulo Freire, development should be people-centric as it is the right of all people to individually and collectively speak their word. "This is not the privilege of some few men, but the right of every (wo)man. Consequently, no one can say a true word alone, nor can he say it for another, in a prescriptive act which robs others of their words", he emphasized.

Since participation is crucial to sharing information, knowledge, trust, commitment and right attitudes for decision-making, the development edifice needs to be woven around people, not people around development. All men, women and children must be at the centre of its attention. At the same time, this development should be sustainable as raising future production may involve sacrifices made in the present.

Participation is closely linked to decentralization. It largely depends upon empowering the poor at times with the central government aid as in *Jan Dhan Yojana* in India. Decentralization or the devolution of power from higher level to the ground level is the essence of democracy. Its success depends on education, accountability and designing appropriate structures and sequences of decision-making. For instance, the Panchayat Act of 1985 in India not only allows for the transfer of development funds from state to the district but also involves people at the grassroots level in planning and implementation activities. The basic unit of empowerment here is the *gram sabha*, or meeting of all voters in the village. This has improved accountability in *aanganwadis*, schools and health clinics.

Thus, development is multi-dimensional. This approach to development is markedly different from the earlier approaches that regarded expansion of economic opportunities as a necessary precondition for development. Over-concentration on single dimension of income alone, says UNDP, is at best an oversimplification and at worst a gross distortion of reality, for high growth rates do no automatically translate into higher levels of human development.

"This requires a firm policy action to forge a closer link between economic growth and human development. Just as economic growth is necessary for human development, human development is critical to economic growth. This two-way link must be at the heart of any enlightened policy action", it adds.

Therefore, income is just one aspect of the choices—and an extremely important one—but it is not the sum total of human existence. The human development index or HDI combines national income with two social indicators—adult literacy and life expectancy—to give a composite measure of human progress. The HDI fully recognizes that the concept of human development is much broader than its measurement. Thus, development today is no longer confined to growth in GNP alone. For instance, there are many countries in Africa and the Gulf, whose HDI rank is 20 or more places lower than their per capita income rank, showing that they have considerable potential to improve their human development levels by spending their incomes better and planning their investment priorities more wisely (Human Development Report, 1991).

Hence, growth is not the end of development, but the absence of growth often is. Growth in numbers alone without improvement in living standards and overall quality of life is meaningless. Health, education, a good physical environment and socio-economic-political freedom to lead a free and independent life—to name a few components of well-being—may be just as important. Stressing the importance of human freedom, the report says: "Human development is incomplete without human freedom. Throughout history, people have been willing to sacrifice their lives to gain national and personal liberty. Thus, any index of human development should give adequate weight to a society's human freedom in pursuit of material and social goals" (Human Development Report, 1991).

Therefore, development is holistic. It is comprehensive and multifaceted in approach. Real development gives precedence to enhancing human well-being over material opulence, to expanding capabilities over maximizing incomes and to enlarging freedoms over optimizing growth. All this is done by the people themselves through active participation in various processes meant to improve and enrich their lives. This holistic approach to development and evolution in life and all human endeavours therein is echoed in the Vedic prayer for well-being and prosperity of the entire mankind:

Aum Sarve bhavantu sukhinaḥ.
Sarve santu nirāmayāḥ.
Sarve bhadrāṇi paśyantu.
Mā kashchit duḥkha bhāgbhavet.
(May all be prosperous and happy,
May all be free from illness,
May all see what is spiritually uplifting,
May no one suffer)

A universal prayer from *Brihadaryanka Upanishad* 1.4.14.

Development is sustainable. It should meet the needs of the present without compromising the ability of the future generations to meet their own needs. This kind of development, says the World Commission on Environment and Development (WCED) Report, has to be seen and felt in terms of improved living conditions, better infrastructure, safety and security of citizens and above all, less polluted greener environment. "The developmental process involves not only changes in the economic structure, it is also interlinked with the entire social, political and cultural fabric of the society. It aims at bringing about qualitative changes leading to an upward movement of the entire social system. Sustainable development is thus guided by the twin objectives of making the end-users or beneficiaries both self-sufficient and self-reliant". This comprehensive approach to human development takes care of all other approaches such as the human resources approach; the basic needs approach and the human welfare approach. The slogan *sabka saath, sabka vikas* aptly sums up the basic principal of this development model that aims at *Sarve Bhavantu Sukhinah,* i.e. let all be prosperous and happy.

Ultimately, development is indeed the key to progress. It is measured in terms of improvement in the lives of the people and strengthening of the individual's and thereby a nation's capacity to deal with the rest of the world. This is the reason why there is a renewed emphasis on imparting various skills that can be useful for sustainable development in the second decade of the 21st century globalized world. These life sustaining skills, according to UNDP, are classified under four heads:

1. Ways of thinking that includes creativity, critical thinking, problem solving, decision-making and learning;
2. Tools for working such as in information and communication technology and information literacy;
3. Ways of working such as communication and collaboration; and,
4. Skills for living in the world such as citizenship, life and career, personal and social responsibility.

Finally, development, like freedom and sovereignty, is indivisible. Its fruits and benefits can be shared, but its progress cannot be allowed to get thwarted. Its pace can slow down, but its momentum cannot be broken. This is why, given the enormous power and reach of the media—both new as well as traditional—it is incumbent upon their practitioners to have a clear understanding of the dynamics of development and related issues. Therefore, the study of development journalism holds a special place in media academics.

As such development can be both cost and labour intensive. Sometimes nations spend the best of their precious human and material resources in developmental projects only to find one day that schools and hospitals are burnt, banks are looted and innocent civilians are mercilessly killed by those who shriek from their rooftops about poverty and backwardness. Development for these jihadi zealots, who treat their womenfolk as baby-making machines, has no meaning or relevance. While they talk about power and self-reliance, they hold the State as their sworn enemy, and are hell bent on radicalizing their minors against the entire humanity with a vengeance. The recent warning to the US President Donald Trump by an eight-year old is evident of this evil mindset that must be fought tooth and nail if the ideal of universal human development is to be realized.

1

Development: An Evolving Concept

Over the years, particularly after the Second World War, development alone has emerged as the sole criterion for measuring a country's economic condition and its standing in the comity of nations. The economic disparities between the poverty-stricken erstwhile colonies and their rich colonial masters graduated to a North-South divide in the Cold War era. This divide was symptomatic of gross inequalities produced by centuries of subjugation, colonization and exploitation. Several attempts to bridge them have yet to yield the desired results.

1.1 Historical Background

For much of the nineteenth century, Britain, on the strength of its vast colonial empire whose sun would never set, had led the rest of the world in industrial production and trade. The scene changed towards the last quarter of the nineteenth century when Germany after its unification in 1871 emerged as a leading power in Europe, both militarily and economically. The USA also emerged as the world's leading industrial nation after the rise of the Big Business and spread of the Railroad after 1870. With its much higher production of coal, pig iron and steel than Germany and Britain put together, it had already become a world power.

The twentieth century witnessed some important changes in the form of two world wars and their aftermath in the form of the Cold War and independence of erstwhile colonies of Asia, Africa and Latin America. In a sense, in 1900, there was already a single world economy. A few highly industrialized countries like the USA, Germany and Britain provided the world's manufactured goods, while the rest of the world that included colonies like India that were mercilessly exploited by the European imperial powers, provided raw material and food, known as the primary products.

The First World War (1914-1915) and its aftermath gave big boost to the American economy. Many countries such as China and states of Latin America which had bought goods from Europe during the war were unable to get hold of supplies as the war disrupted the trade. This compelled them to buy goods from the USA and Japan, a practice that continued even after the war. Consequently, the USA became the 'economic winner' of the First World War. It became even richer on account of interest on war loans it had provided to Britain and her allies. It also provided loans to Germany to pay its war reparations.

By the end of the Second World War (1939-45), while the economy of the war-ravaged Europe stagnated, the USA was booming as it switched to producing consumer goods which had been in short supply during the war. It was then producing 43 percent of the world iron ore, 45 percent of the crude steel, 60 percent of the railway locomotives and 74 percent of the motor vehicles. It was also the only country in the world rich enough to provide financial aid to Western Europe to recover from war damages.

1.2 The Cold War

Towards the end of the Second World War, relations between Soviet Union and the West became difficult. The bonhomie that had existed between the USSR, the USA and Britain gave way to old suspicions. Relations between the Soviet Russia and the West became worse. Although no actual direct fight took place between the two rival camps, the period after 1945 marked the beginning of the first phase of what is known as the Cold War. The Cold War never saw any open conflict between the hostile powers. Instead they attacked each other with propaganda, counter economic measures and non-cooperation.

In a way, the Cold War epitomized the ideological conflict between communism and capitalism. The communist system of organizing the state and society was based on the ideas of Karl Marx who believed that the wealth of a country should be collectively owned and shared by everybody. The economy should be centrally planned and the interests and the well-being of the working classes be safeguarded by state social policies. The capitalist system, on the other hand, operates on the basis of private ownership of a country's wealth. The driving forces behind capitalism are private enterprise for making profits and the preservation of the power of private wealth.

Consequently, after 1945, the world split into capitalist and communist blocs. The two super-powers, the USA and the USSR, gathered allies around themselves. The liberal-democratic capitalist bloc consisted of the highly developed industrial nations—the USA, Canada, Western Europe, Japan, Australia and New Zealand. They believed in private enterprise and private ownership of wealth with profit as the great motivating influence with minimum of state interference. In contrast, the authoritarian communist bloc believed in state controlled, centrally planned economies to eliminate the negative fall out of capitalism in the form of slumps, unemployment and the unequal distribution of wealth. It consisted of the erstwhile Soviet Union along with its satellite states in Eastern Europe and later, China, North Korea and North Vietnam.

The Cold War raged full swing with the communist takeover of Czechoslovakia in February 1948. The Berlin blockade (June 1948-May 1949) and the subsequent formation of the North Atlantic Treaty Organization (NATO) in April 1949 brought the Cold War to its first climax. Formation of NATO was a very significant development and Stalin took it as a challenge. This led to the onset of a nuclear arms race between the two superpowers when in September 1949 the USSR successfully exploded an atomic bomb and the USA responded by producing a hydrogen bomb many times more powerful than the atomic bomb. Subsequently, the USSR also developed its own hydrogen bomb. Things worsened when the USSR and communist China signed a treaty of alliance in February 1950 and a few months later in June the same year, the troops from communist North Korea invaded non-communist South Korea.

The Cold War continued despite several thaws. The death of Stalin in 1953 brought forward new Russian leadership in Malenkov, Bulganin and Khruschev. They all wanted to improve relations with the USA as they knew very well that any further escalation in tension would lead to an all out self-destructive nuclear war. In February 1956, Khruschev outlined his policy of 'peaceful co-existence' with the West, something that China never liked as Mao saw in it as a deviation from the Marxist-Leninist position. Nevertheless, the ice between the superpower relations began to melt and led to the removal of occupation forces from Austria in 1955. However, Germany remained divided and tensions mounted over Vietnam and the Cuban missile crisis in 1962. The nuclear arms race continued well into the 1970s.

Thus, the decades of 1960s to the 1970s saw the rise and fall of détente as the US and the Soviet Union made efforts to avoid nuclear confrontation. Moscow faced hostility in the satellite states in Europe as well as from Beijing proving the fact that the vast region from Beijing to Berlin was not a monolithic bloc. In 1961, Albania left the Warsaw Pact while Romania wanted to follow suit. In 1965, there was an open opposition in Armenia and Ukraine, known as the food bowl of the Soviet Union. In early 1968, Czechoslovakia led by Alexander Dubcek, the secretary of the Communist Party there, launched a programme of 'reforms' with a view to establish 'socialism with human face'. This was strongly resisted by the USSR. He was replaced by Gustav Husak in 1969 who accepted the dictates from Moscow and managed to continue until 1987.

Meanwhile, in response to this development, Brezhnev, in an article in Pravda, outlined the Soviet policy in an article entitled "Sovereignty and International Obligations of Socialist Countries'. He said that communist countries must subordinate their independence to the interests of all communist countries and to the entire communist movement as defined by the Soviet Union. This became known as 'the Brezhnev Doctrine'. On August 22, 1968, the Security Council of the United Nations passed a resolution condemning armed intervention in Czechoslovakia and called for withdrawal of the Warsaw Pact forces from there.

Meanwhile, the rift between Moscow and Beijing continued to widen. Mao, who was already critical of the Soviet policy of peaceful co-existence with the liberal-democratic West, did not appreciate Khruschev's attack on 'the cult of personality' and scrapped the Second Five Year Plan to adopt a new programme called the 'Great Leap Forward' in 1958. The programme failed miserably and Russia responded by abruptly recalling 1,300 advisors and military technicians from China who left behind numerous unfinished tasks. China also felt slighted when Moscow did not extend sufficient support for recovering Taiwan. While the Soviet Union was busy in the Cuban Missile Crisis, the Chinese army attacked India's North-East frontier and Ladakh on October 20, 1962. Despite ups and downs in Russia-China relations, their basic commitment to communist ideology kept them together. This became quite clear when India sought assistance from Russia against unprovoked Chinese aggression, Moscow denied any help saying: India may be a friend, but China is a brother.

However, dissatisfaction with the communist system began to grow and within the short period from mid-1988 to the end of 1991, communism collapsed, under its own weight, first in Eastern Europe and then in the USSR. Poland was the first to reject communism, closely followed by Hungary and East Germany and the rest. The two German states were reunited in October 1990. The Berlin Wall that separated them came down in 1989 and the unified Germany emerged as the most powerful state in Europe. The August 1991 coup in Moscow led to the break-up of the Soviet Union by the year-end. With the disintegration of the once mighty USSR, communism finally swept away even in Russia.

1.3 Truman Doctrine and the Marshall Plan

In March 1947, the US President Harry S. Truman had announced that the US 'would support free people who are resisting subjugation by armed minorities or by outside pressure'. By 1949, the communists, who were trying to overthrow monarchy in Greece, were defeated. Turkey, which too was reeling under a similar threat from the communists, received massive US aid of about 60 million dollars to keep itself intact. Thus, the Truman Doctrine made it clear that the US was committed to the policy of containing communism, not just in Europe, but throughout the world, including Korea and Vietnam.

1.3.1 The Marshall Plan: Named after the American Secretary of State, George Marshall, it was an economic extension of the Truman Doctrine. Announced in June 1947, it was a name given to the European Recovery Programme or ERP which offered economic and financial help wherever it was needed. 'Our policy', said Marshall, 'is directed not against any country or doctrine, but against hunger, poverty, desperation and chaos'. During the next four years, over 13,000 million dollars of Marshall Aid under the Marshall Plan was poured into war devastated Western Europe for its reconstruction and economic stability through recovery of agriculture and industry.

Although this aid was theoretically available for Eastern Europe and Czechoslovakia wanted it badly to ease its food shortage, Russian foreign minister Molotov decried it as 'dollar imperialism' and a blatant interference in Eastern Europe which Stalin considered to be a Russian sphere of influence. As a result, not only the USSR and her satellite states rejected it, even

Czechoslovakia, the only remaining democratic state in Eastern Europe and a bridge between east and west was taken over by the communists in February 1948.

1.3.2 The Molotov Plan: Thanks to the Marshall Aid, in early 1948, the economic prosperity of the three Western zones of Berlin that were merged to form a single economic unit, stood in sharp contrast to the poverty of the Russian zone. Therefore, in response to the Marshall Aid, Stalin in 1949, announced the Molotov Plan to offer Russian aid to her satellites. Under the plan, Eastern Europe was to be industrialized, collectivized and centralized. All the communist states were expected to trade primarily within the members of Cominform, an organization set up by Stalin to draw together the various European communist parties.

Another organization known as Comecon (Council of Mutual Economic Assistance) was also set up to coordinate their economic policies to convert them into a single integrated economy. Thus, the Molotov Plan was the first Russian-sponsored step towards an economically united Eastern Bloc. All the satellite states were to be a carbon copy of the USSR with the same political, economic and educational systems and the same Five Year Plans. All had to carry out the bulk of their trade with Russia. Under the Warsaw Pact of 1955, their foreign policies and armed forces were controlled from Moscow.

1.4 The Third World

Aftermath of the Second World War saw a wave of decolonization and revolution in the erstwhile colonies and mandates of the West European powers in Asia, Africa and Latin America. The culmination of liberation struggles and the emergence of sovereign countries completely transformed the political map of the world. The number of internationally recognized states in Asia quintupled. In Africa, where there had been one in 1939, there were now about fifty. Even in the Americas, where early nineteenth century decolonization had left twenty or so Latino republics, decolonization added another dozen.

Together these undeveloped or underdeveloped countries, whose number rapidly grew during the 1950s and 1960s, comprised the Third World, a phrase coined by French economic historian, Alfred Sauvy, in 1952. It was used to describe countries which were not part of the First World comprising industrialized capitalist nations to the west of the Iron Curtain and the Second World comprising the communist bloc of the Soviet Union and its satellite states in East Europe. However, the position of China remained ambiguous. Some grouped it under the Second World as it was communist while others associated it with the countries of the South because it was associated initially with the Non-Aligned Movement. By 1970, the Third World consisted of Africa, Asia (except the USSR and China), Latin America and the Middle East. With the fall of the Iron Curtain following the disintegration of the Soviet Union in 1991, the phrase Third World also lost any specificity. Today, it continues to denote the poor and undeveloped countries of the world and the implications of this phrase are widely understood.

Comprising over two-thirds of the earth's land surface and home to about three-fourth of world's population, the Third World had less than one-fifth share in world's income. Even basic necessities of subsistence such as minimum food, clothing and shelter were not easily accessible to the poor masses. They led a hopelessly miserable life of poverty, malnutrition, disease and illiteracy. The reason for this mass poverty and low living standards was and continues to be found in their stagnating or slow growing economies and rapidly growing population.

1.4.1 The Indian Experience: Ironically, the extreme poverty and underdevelopment of the Third World, including India, was not a natural phenomenon. It was caused by their relentless exploitation by their colonial masters who pinned them down to the state of underdevelopment and forced them to remain de-industrialized by draining out their natural resources and raw materials for factories in Manchester and other European cities.

"It was not the policy of the East India Company to foster Indian industries...As early as 1769, the Directors (of the Company) wished the manufacturers of raw silk to be encouraged in Bengal, and that of silk fabrics discouraged. And they also directed that silk-winders should be made to work in the Company's factories, and prohibited from working outside 'under severe penalties, by the authority of the Government'. This mandate had its desired effect. The manufacturing of silk and cotton goods declined in India, and the people who had exported these goods to the markets of Europe and Asia in previous centuries began to import them in increasing quantities". [1]

Despite decline of industries and manufactures in Bengal and Madras due to repeated famines, the constant and never-ending barrage of inquiries about how British goods could be forced on the people of India continued. "The supplies of trade", according to Warren Hastings, "are for the wants and luxuries of a people; the poor in India may be said to have no wants. Their wants are confined to their dwellings, to their food, and to a scanty portion of clothing, all of which they can have from the soil that they tread upon". [2]

The condition of Indian agriculture under British rule was even worse. "Agriculture is now virtually the only remaining source of national wealth in India, and four-fifths of the Indian people depend on it. But the land tax levied by the British Government is not only excessive, but, what is worse, it is fluctuating and uncertain in many provinces...In India, the State has fostered no new industries and revived no old industries for the people; on the other hand, it intervenes at each recurring land settlement to take what it considers its where out of the produce of the soil", wrote Dutt, one of the first Indians to get into Indian Civil Service.

Discussing the causes of Indian poverty and the lack of progress he wrote: "For one who has himself spent the best and happiest years of his life in the work of Indian administration, it is an ungracious and a painful task to dwell on the weak side of that administration, and the financial and economic policy of the Indian Government. I have undertaken this duty because at the present moment the economic story of British India has to be told, and the deep-seated cause of the poverty of the Indian people has to be explained. Place any other country under the same condition, with crippled industries, with agriculture subject to a heavy and uncertain land tax, and with financial arrangements requiring one-half of its revenues to be annually remitted out of the country, and the most prosperous nation on earth will soon know the horrors of famine". [3]

Hence, the socio-economic deprivation of countries like India was a result of ruthless oppressive policies of the imperialist powers. However, this was not the case before the start of colonialism when on account of being plough using agricultural communities China, India, the Middle East, and Europe were at the same level of development. By 1945, while much of Asia, Africa and the Middle East remained predominantly agricultural, the imperialist powers like England, France and the Netherlands, had turned into mighty industrial giants. No wonder then that Europe on the strength of its massive loot and plunder of its colonies was the first to emerge as an industrial force, a fact that not only crippled whatever little industry existed in their former colonies like India but also decelerated their growth by a couple of centuries. Clearly, poverty and backwardness of the erstwhile colonies, including India, was a legacy of centuries of subjugation under foreign yoke and British colonialism.

As a result, the economic disparities between the poverty-stricken erstwhile colonies and their rich colonial masters not only widened but also graduated to a North-South divide in the post-war years. According to the 1980 Brandt Report on the

Third World Problems, prepared by a group of world leaders under the chairmanship of West German Chancellor Willy Brandt, the world could be roughly divided into two parts, the North and the South. The North comprised the developed industrial nations of North America, Europe, the USSR, and Japan, plus Australia and New Zealand. The countries of Asia, Africa and Latin America which were 'non-industrialized', 'underdeveloped' or 'developing' comprised the South. The report defined 'the South' thus: "in general terms, and although neither is a uniform or permanent grouping, "North" and "South" are broadly synonymous with "rich" and "poor", "developed" and "developing". [4] This division was later reinforced by the South Commission, adding, 'while countries of the North are, by and large, in control of their destinies, those of the South are very vulnerable to external factors and lacking in functioning sovereignty'. [5]

1.5 Characteristics of the Third World

Unlike the highly developed and industrialized OECD countries of the West, the developing countries of the Third World were ranked by their levels of gross national income (GNI) per capita as low-income countries (LICs), lower-middle-income countries (LMCs) and upper-middle-income countries (UMCs). All of them, irrespective of their GNI, shared low levels of human development, including health and education.

As a result, the underdeveloped Third World remained mired in extreme poverty, uncontrolled population, malnutrition, infant mortality, disease, illiteracy, unemployment, rampant corruption and sharp inequalities in social, political and economic life. All these problems, in one way or the other, are linked to the basic problem of uncontrolled population. It has been seen that all social, economic and environmental problems of cities and rural areas are aggravated by the rapid population growth in less developed nations. This trend, which began after the Second

World War, remains unabated to this day and is causing high birth rates resulting in massive population growth.

Despite notable exceptions like the BRICS economies, almost the entire developing world continues to grapple with low levels of income and living, low levels of productivity, high rate of population growth, high and rising levels of unemployment as well as underemployment and high dependence on agriculture and other primary production. This is in sharp contrast to life in developed nations where all broad indicators of human development such as life expectancy at birth, expected years of schooling, mean years of schooling, per capita gross national product (GNP) show a healthy trend towards growth and prosperity.

Thus, judged by the criterion of development economics that defines development as a process involving elimination of poverty, income inequality and unemployment, under development of these countries is a situation full of deprivations and disadvantages. In terms of poverty, "underdevelopment is a real fact of life for over three billion people in the world". [6] Therefore, the poverty trap in which the developing world finds itself so badly caught is itself a product of vicious nexus between poverty and uncontrolled population. In fact, uncontrolled population is the mother of all the problems that plague the developing world today. Their high population growth rates are directly proportional to their high misery index. This broad commonality transcends the inherent diversity of all the developing countries. Economists like Todaro have therefore identified 10 common traits that characterize their lot. They are as under:

1.5.1 Lower Levels of Living and Productivity: The vicious nexus between poverty-population results in extremely low levels of living and productivity. Low income leads to low investment in education and health as well as plant and equipment and infrastructure, which in turn leads to low productivity and economic stagnation. Thus, throughout the developing world, levels of labour productivity are extremely low compared with those in developed countries. Low level of living and low productivity are self-reinforcing social and economic phenomenon in the Third World countries and as such, according to Mydral, are the principal manifestation of, and contributors to, their development.

1.5.2 Low Levels of Human Capital: Despite progress, a majority of Third World countries miserably lag behind in human capital—health, education and skills—which is vital to economic growth and human development. Their average levels of nutrition, life expectancy and literacy remain dismally low. As compared to developed countries, the child and maternal mortality ratio continues to be extremely high. The under-five mortality is still 15 times higher in low-income countries than in high-income countries. Similarly, high levels of illiteracy, low schooling attainment and under-nourishment continue to plague countries like India.

1.5.3 High Rate of Population Growth and Dependency Burden: By all accounts, high growth rate in population is both the cause and effect of poverty that stems from underdevelopment. However, there is a growing feeling that underdevelopment, in this context, can be a state of a country as well as mind. People with saner minds try to limit their family size for the well-being of their children and the country as a whole. But those who are aware, yet do not practice family planning because their religion does not allow it, not only betray the best interests of their near and dear ones, but also of their country. And, given the strong linkages between uncontrolled population and poverty, those who do not believe in controlling population, should accept poverty and the resultant backwardness as their fate accompli. They should, therefore, stop complaining about their backwardness and also stop seeking undue favours from the State.

1.5.4 Higher Levels of Inequality and Absolute Poverty: Both poverty and inequality are the results as well as causes of slower and distorted growth. The cycle of low productivity, low income and the resultant slow growth in underdeveloped countries has led to the theory of "circular and cumulative causation" by Nobel Laureate Gunnar Mydral. Greater the absolute poverty, greater the inequality as is evident in both sub-Saharan Africa and South Asia.

1.5.5 Social Fragmentation: Poverty, high population rate, underdevelopment and backwardness cause social fragmentation. The most fascinating example of this is India. Ask any 21st century Indian what is he/she? And, the answer would be—well, I am a Bengali; I am from Tamilnaad; no, I am a Malyali; Na na asi Punjabi haan!...Nooooo, I am a Muslim, can't you see! Probe a little further and the answer would be: Yes, I am a Brahmin, I am an SC/ST, I am a dalit, I am a minority! The list is endless. But rarely, yes rarely, would you come across an individual, except of course, a brave army jawan, who would say: I am an Indian, a proud Indian first, everything else later.

Therefore, uneven economic growth and development have not only accentuated regional disparities but also sharpened inequalities. Even the policy of caste-based reservation has not helped in removing these inequalities. Clamour for economic benefits under reservations have fragmented Indian society to such an extent that a collective sense of national identity and national pride is virtually lost in the maze of sub-identities. This weakness has become India's Achilles heel. It is being exploited by anti-social, anti-national separatists and nefarious elements. It is high time to understand that just as a citizen of England is English first, a Catholic or Protestant later, likewise every citizen of India or Hindustan is an Indian first irrespective of his or her caste, creed, religion and region.

1.5.6 Larger Rural Population but Rapid Rural-to-Urban Migration: Poor and backward rural areas are not only densely populated but also out of sync with the developed urban centres. The urban centres have infrastructure, basic amenities like food, water and electricity. They also have services and job opportunities. All these things result in non-stop migration from rural areas to the urban.

At one point in time, India was known for its brain drain. Its best brains—the highly educated youth—were moving to the West in search of greener pastures. Today, this trend might have reversed or slowed down, but the rural-urban migration has not. This needs to be stemmed by providing basic amenities, adequate support system, creating infrastructure and employment opportunities for the rural masses. Rural development therefore is the need of the hour.

1.5.7 Substantial Dependence on Agricultural Production and Lower Levels of Industrialization and Manufactured Exports: The developing countries are heavily dependent on agricultural production as the vast majority of their population lives in rural areas. This is because in less developed countries, agriculture is often characterized by primitive technologies, poor organization and limited physical and human capital inputs. In contrast, industrialization, a hallmark of modernization and economic power, is associated with high productivity and incomes.

Regarding exports, the developing countries, particularly those in Africa, continue to heavily rely on primary exports from agricultural and mineral sectors. It is the middle income economies that are swiftly catching up with the developed world in the share of manufactured goods in their exports. This is despite the fact that neither the quality of goods being exported nor the technology used is as high and advanced as that of the developed world.

1.5.8 Underdeveloped Financial and Other Markets: In the absence of well-defined and well-entrenched legal and institutional systems, the less developed countries are often financially unstable. This is on account of their imperfect markets, especially financial markets; lack of legal system that enforces contracts and validates property rights; lack of a stable and trustworthy currency as well as a well-developed system of banking and insurance; absence of infrastructural support and low creditworthiness of potential borrowers. This is why international credit agencies like the IMF and the World Bank insist on 'stabilization and structural adjustment programme' in these countries as a necessary precondition for credit availability to ward off default on debt as it happened in India in 1991.

1.5.9 Lingering Colonial Impacts: The 157 developing nations of Africa, Asia and Latin America were either former colonies or mandates of the West European imperial powers. Their relentless exploitation by colonizers decelerated their economic development by a couple of centuries. They were de-industrialized by draining out their natural resources and raw materials and driven to the state of underdevelopment. This situation continues to persist despite efforts to improve their lot.

1.5.10 External Dependence: The underdeveloped Third World continues to suffer on account of its heavy dependence on the developed world. This dependence stems from its low influence and weak bargaining power in the comity of nations. For instance, agreements within the World Trade Organization (WTO) that favoured agricultural subsidies in rich countries harmed their farmers. Likewise, one-sided regulations of intellectual property rights (IPRs) have been unfavourable to the developing countries. Many countries, including India, have suffered on account of biased patents regime. According to Todaro, "the phenomenon of underdevelopment needs to be viewed in a national and international context. Economic and social forces, both internal and external, are responsible for the poverty, inequality and low productivity that commonly characterize most Third World nations". [7]

1.6 Development: The Conceptual Framework

Amidst all this confusion, GNP alone became the sole criteria for measuring a country's economic condition and its standing in the comity of nations. The GNP-centric concept of development missed out on the social dimension of development as it did not pay attention to the human factor in overall development. It was inspired by the Western industrialization process that laid stress on modernization at the expense of tradition and culture. It emphasized capital infusion and diffusion of modern innovations for industrialization and urbanization that were considered critical for industry-driven national growth. All this was done at the cost of agriculture to prioritize industrialization.

The initial years of development also saw the birth of multilateral development assistance in 1945 to assist developing economies. This included International Monetary Fund or IMF, the World Bank and the United Nations with its special agencies. In 1949 emerged the bilateral development assistance in the form of Truman's Point Four Programme whose outcome was called development.

1.6.1 Point Four Programme of 1949: It provided the much-needed impetus to ameliorate the pathetic condition of the toiling millions of the poor South. The sheer magnitude of the problems of undeveloped and underdeveloped Third World caught the attention of the then US President Harry S. Truman who saw in it an opportunity to win th 'hearts and minds' of the developing world where "more than half of the people of the world are living in conditions approaching misery", he said, adding: "Their food is inadequate. They are victims of disease. Their economic life is primitive and stagnant. Their poverty is a threat both to them and to more prosperous areas. For the first time in history, humanity has the knowledge and skill to relieve the suffering of these people. The United States is pre-eminent among nations in the development of industrial and scientific techniques. The material resources which we can afford to use for assistance of other peoples are limited. But our imponderable resources in technical knowledge are constantly growing and are inexhaustible".

In his oft-quoted and much applauded inaugural speech of January 20, 1949, President Truman proposed a 'technical assistance programme' as the fourth objective of the US foreign policy. "We must embark on a bold new programme for making the benefits of our scientific advances and industrial progress available for the improvement and growth of underdeveloped areas", he said. [8]

This programme, meant to share the US know-how under the '1949 Point Four Programme', was aimed at 'greater production' through "a wider and more vigorous application of modern scientific and technical knowledge in agriculture, commerce, industry and health. The old imperialism—exploitation for foreign profit—has no place in our plans. What we envisage is a programme of development based on the concepts of democratic fair-dealing. All countries, including our own, will greatly benefit from a constructive programme for the better use of the world's human and natural resources", said President Truman in his speech which is considered to be the beginning of the modern conception of development as it synthesized the world divided between the prosperous North and the poor South.

The emergent concept of development that aimed at modernization of traditional societies was defined "as a type of social change in which new ideas are introduced into a social system in order to produce higher per capita incomes and levels of living through more modern production methods and improved social organization. [9] This conception was very much in line with what President Truman had said: 'The key to prosperity and peace is greater production through a wider and more vigorous application of modern scientific and technical knowledge". [10]

Truman's address had an electrifying effect. The industrialized West readily agreed to join hands. The UN and its various executing agencies went ahead full throttle to provide every possible input—be it investment capital, industrial plant, agricultural methods or entrepreneurial training to the recently decolonized and newly independent countries of Asia, Africa and Latin America. In the words of noted communication scholar Daniel Lerner, the decade of the 1950s witnessed the spread of economic development projects around much of the world. This process of reviving cultures, emerging nations, and new states was widely characterized as a "revolution of rising expectations". [11]

"People throughout the backward and impoverished areas of the world suddenly acquired the sense that a better life was possible for them. New leaders arose who encouraged their people to believe in the immanence of progress and the fulfilment of their new, often millennial hopes. A great forward surge of expectancy and aspiration, of desire and demand, was awakened during the past decade among peoples who for centuries had remained hopeless and inert. This forward feeling was shared by those of us whose unchanging task is to understand". [12] This marked the beginning of the modernization paradigm.

1.7 The Modernization Approach

The concept of development cantered round the idea of modernization of traditional societies through technology and concomitant process of industrialization. The proponents of modernization paradigm took development of the poor, backward and underdeveloped Third World as a challenge. Their task was to bring the underdeveloped countries out of the dungeon of poverty by promoting economic growth with the help of free-market approaches. In this exercise, they identified, among other things, two main reasons for underdevelopment such as:

1. A biased social structure which suffered from a top-heavy land tenure system and an inefficient and slow government machinery; and
2. Traditional behaviour and attitude among the masses that acted as obstacles to modernization. [13]

Thus, change was a necessary precondition to bring about desired transformation of a traditional society into a modern one. The change basically worked on four levels namely cultural, technocratic, political and economic. At the cultural level, it meant an absolute rejection of the traditional belief system which was considered an impediment to modernization and adoption of attitudes and behaviours favourable to innovations and modernity. At the technocratic level, it meant going for capital-intensive heavy industries and rejection of labour-intensive projects and sectors. At the political level, instead of joining either the US or the Soviet Union, the Third World countries preferred to remain equidistant and forged their own alliance in the name of non-alignment. Economically, it meant either joining the capitalist or the communist bloc.

1.7.1 Passing of Traditional Society: "At the technocratic level, modernization required people with inquisitive minds who were guided by faith in the scientific method and rooted in the principles of enlightenment. At the political level, it required staunch advocates of the doctrine of liberalism based on the political freedom and the adoption of democratic systems. Finally, at the economic level, it required blind faith in the virtues and power of the free market, with no or minimal government intervention", writes Lerner, in his magnum opus, The Passing of Traditional Society, 1958.

However, to the critics of modernization, the process had two aspects. One was the dynamic, progressive, forward-looking, and promising unprecedented abundance, freedom and fulfilment. The other was grim, revealing new problems arising out of the very efficiency of the instruments it had created, as also problems of alienation, poverty and pollution amidst rapid urbanization and boom in materialism unleashed by the whirlwind of market forces.

1.7.2 Social Mobilization: The concept of development through modernization is rooted in the idea of modernity that characterizes modern societies. It refers to the sense or the idea that the present is discontinuous with the past and that, through a process of social and cultural change, life in the present is fundamentally different from that in the past. Essentially, it is a world of change marked by an ability to confront the new without rushing to the defence of tradition. According to noted social philosopher Jurgen Habermas, modernity is essentially a mode of thought that refuses to accept tradition unreflectively.

"It is a world of the present, adrift from tradition and bound for the future", he said.

Central to this modernization approach is the concept of social mobilization defined by Karl Deutsch as "the process in which old social, economic and psychological commitments are eroded and broken and people become available for new patterns of socialization and behaviour". [14] It is rooted in the evolutionary concept of Darwin to social change that inspired and informed the dominant paradigm in the West vis-à-vis development in the Third world. It held that social mobilization was able to generate continuing change. It was also able to absorb the stress of change and adapt itself to changing demand. "In other words, the process seemed relatively irreversible. Once the necessary conditions were established for take-off, a country took off, became modern, and stayed modern". [15]

A key barrier to overcome was the traditional personality of the people in the Third Word. This personality, as delineated by Rogers in the 'Sub-culture of Peasantry', was characterized by traits such as low esteem, authoritarian values, resistance to innovation, fatalism and non-achievement. Thus, the traditional societies needed complete transformation in terms of psychological and social change by imparting modern values, skills and techniques.

1.7.3 The Modern State: The idea of a modern state within modernization paradigm was based on the presumption that a nation became truly modern and developed when it arrived at that point where it closely resembled Western industrial nations in terms of political and economic behaviour and institutions, attitude towards technology and innovation, and social and psychic mobility. [16] Within this narrative, the development of an individual was defined as "the process by which individuals change from a traditional way of life to a more complex, technologically advanced, and rapidly changing style of life" by Rogers.

The modernization paradigm of development was grounded in the neo-classical economic theory that followed the route of economic growth through industrialization. It measured growth by gross national produce (GNP) rates and by the 'encouragement of all factors and institutions that accelerated and maintained high growth in areas such as capital-intensive industrialization and technology with private ownership of factors of production, free trade, and the principle of laissez-faire'. [17] It gave complete freedom to capitalists and entrepreneurs with minimal governmental interference. The government's job was confined to maintaining law and order and providing good climate for higher production.

This theory was based on the economic model that was successfully tried and tested in the resuscitation of war-ravaged Western Europe under the Marshall Plan. The Marshall Plan was announced by the United States in June 1947 for the economic recovery of Europe.

Under this, all West European countries received massive financial aid. The aim behind this was not only to help in the economic recovery of Europe and to enable the American economy to recover, but also to keep the communists at bay within the confines of the 'Iron Curtain'. Interestingly, the phrase 'Iron Curtain' was used by British Prime Minister Winston Churchill in a speech at Fulton, Missouri (USA) in March 1946, when he said: "From Stettin in the Baltic to Trieste in the Adriatic, an iron curtain has descended across the continent".

To counter it, the Soviet Union extended economic aid to the East European countries under the Molotov Plan. The economies of the Eastern Bloc countries were subordinated to the Soviet economy by creating a series of joint ventures and by the imposition of Soviet style Five Year Plans to promote heavy industry while the agriculture was partially collectivized.

Endnotes

1. Dutt, Romesh (1960), "The Economic History of India: Under Early British Rule 1757-1837", Vol. I, Ministry of Information and Broadcasting, Government of India; New Delhi, p. 176.
2. Ibid.
3. Ibid.
4. Brandt Commission Report, 1981, p. 31.
5. South Commission, 1990, p. 1.
6. Todaro, P. Michael (2013), "Economic Development", New Delhi, Pearson.
7. Ibid.
8. Daniels, Walter M. (1951), "The Four Point Programme", New York: H.W. Wilson.
9. Rogers, Everett, M. (1969), p. 18.
10. Daniels, Walter M. (1951), "The Point Four Programme", New York; H.W. Wilson.
11. Lerner, Daniel (2010), "Toward a Communication Theory of Modernization", in Daya Kishan Thussu (ed.), 'International Communication: A Reader', Routledge; London, p. 75.
12. Ibid.
13. Rogers, Everett, M., 1976.
14. Schramm, Wilbur (1976),"End of an Old Paradigm", in W. Schramm and D. Lerner (eds.), 'Communication and Change', Honolulu: East-West Centre, The University Press of Hawaii.
15. Ibid.
16. Fjes, Fred (1976), paper on 'Communication and Development', College of Communications, University of Illinois, Urbana-Champaign.
17. Melkote, S.R. (2010), "Theories of Development Communication" in Daya Kishan Thussu (ed.), 'International Communication: A Reader', Routledge; London, p. 106.

2

Shifting Goalposts of Development

Since its early formulation in 1949, the concept of development has been evolving constantly. It has been subjected to intense scrutiny to accommodate shifting goalposts to achieve holistic and sustainable development by ensuring economic growth along with equality, freedom and social justice.

2.1 Period of Great Optimism

The Truman Doctrine and the subsequent Point Four Programme of 1949 that provided the early conceptual framework of development ushered in a period of great optimism. It was characterized by the Dominant Paradigm of Development that advocated economic growth through industrialization and urbanization with the help of capital-intensive technology. It banked on centralized economic planning for development and put the onus of underdevelopment on the internal problems of a country such as biased social structure as well as traditional attitudes and behaviour of the masses that constrained development. It strongly recommended modernization through rapid industrialization which was a tried and tested remedy for the post-war recovery of Western Europe. It heavily relied on diffusion of modernizing innovations for development.

Wilbur Schramm, another key modernization theorist, hailed the role of mass media in development in his influential book, 'Mass Media and National Development', published in 1964 in conjunction with UNESCO. He saw the mass media as a 'bridge to a wider world', as the vehicle for transferring new ideas and models from the North to the South and, within the South, from urban to rural areas. "The task of mass media of information and the 'new media' of education is to speed and ease the long, slow social transformation required for economic development, and, in particular, to speed and smooth the task of modernizing human resources behind the national effort", he said. [1]

As a result, this period saw the dominance of mass media in the development discourse. Mass media were hailed as 'magic multipliers' of development benefits through their direct, powerful and uniform impact. They were considered as agents and indices of modernization. They were seen as the vehicles for transferring new ideas and models from the West to the Third World and from urban areas to rural countryside. They were the tools to usher in social change by ushering a climate of modernization.

The strength of the mass media lay in their one-way, top-down, simultaneous and wide dissemination of information which was a missing link in the development chain. The powerful role of mass media in modernization led to setting up of standards for minimum criteria of media availability for development in developing countries.

2.2 Growth versus Development

Till the 1960s, the concept of development was confined to economic growth measured in terms of gross national product or GNP or GDP i.e. gross domestic product with rates varying from five percent to seven percent or more. It was widely held that economic growth could be easily realized by mobilizing resources and raising their productivity. However, as compared to economic growth, the concept of economic development is a broader and more comprehensive one. In his book, 'Economic Development' (1965), noted economist, C.P. Kindleberger had said: "Whereas economic growth merely refers to a rise in output, economic development implies changes in technological and institutional organization of production as well as distributive pattern of income". Although, in some underdeveloped countries, the process of economic growth has been accompanied by economic development, but this has only been taken as an exception, not as a rule.

The decades of 1950s and 1960s, saw a few developing countries achieve their economic growth targets. Yet, their living conditions remained abysmally poor. Rise in GNP failed to mitigate poverty and its attendant problems like unemployment and inequality. It failed to transform their traditional societies from backward to modern. All this caused widespread dejection and disillusionment with the narrow concept of development based on GNP. The Third World countries, in their zeal to remove poverty and improve economic condition, started agitating for a direct attack on 'widespread absolute poverty'. This led to the revision of the development concept.

In the 1970s, economic development was redefined within the context of a growing economy. Economists in the developed world grudgingly conceded that while there can be growth without development, development without growth is unconceivable. Also, a substantial rise in a country's GNP is required before it can hope to expand its industrial and service sectors. In fact, nowhere in the world has the occupational distribution of population changed in the absence of growth. Therefore, unlike economic growth, the process of development was seen as far more extensive and complex as it involves changes in the composition of output as well as a shift in the allocation of productive resources. This is needed to ensure social justice through equitable distribution of benefits of development.

Thus, economic development was redefined to include improvements in material welfare, especially for persons with the lowest incomes, the eradication of mass poverty with its correlates of illiteracy, disease and early death, changes in the composition of inputs and outputs that generally include shifts in the underlying structure of production away from agricultural towards industrial activities, the organization of the economy in such a way that productive employment is generally among the working age population rather than the situation of a privileged minority and the correspondingly greater participation of broadly based groups in making decisions about the direction, economic and otherwise, in which they should move to improve their welfare. [2]

Later, in his critique of the development paradigm, renowned economist Denis Goulet, provided a valuable insight into the real purpose of development. According to him, [3] at least three basic components as core values should serve as a conceptual basis and practical guidelines for understanding the 'inner' meaning of development. These core values—sustenance, self-esteem and freedom—represent common goals sought by all individuals and societies. They relate to fundamental human needs that find their expression in almost all societies and cultures.

- Sustenance: The life-sustaining basic human needs include food, shelter, health and protection. When any of these is absent or in critically short supply, a condition of absolute 'underdevelopment' exists.
- Self-esteem: Also known as a sense of worth and self-respect, self-esteem, according to Goulet, is the second universal component of good life.
- Freedom: Freedom to lead a life free from subservience should be the third most important goal of development, Goulet said while stressing what Arthur Lewis, the pioneer of development economics, had earlier said: "The advantage of economic growth is not that wealth increases happiness, but that it increases the range of human choice". [4]

Lewis had, as early as 1955, emphasized that the appropriate objective of development is 'increasing the range of human choice'. However, he chose to concentrate particularly on 'the growth of output per head' since that 'gives man greater control over his environment and thereby increases his freedom'.

Later, not only the concept of freedom was incorporated in the World Development Report of 1990, but it was also enlarged to encompass various components of freedom such as political freedom, freedom of expression, political participation and equality of opportunity.

This inclusive view of the nature of economic development nailed the trickle-down theory which saw development as purely an economic phenomenon in which rapid gains from the overall growth of GNP and per capita income would automatically trickle-down to bring benefits to the masses in the form of jobs and other economic opportunities. The main preoccupation is, therefore, to get the growth job done while problems of poverty, unemployment, and income distribution are perceived to be of secondary importance.

2.3 Period of Pessimism

As expected, the decade of the 1970s turned out to be a period of deep pessimism characterized by widespread disappointment with the rate and nature of development. By the earlier definition of growth, many underdeveloped countries were developing, but by the new criteria of poverty, inequality and unemployment, they were not. Many such countries which experienced relatively high rates of growth of per capita income during the previous two decades, hardly showed any decline in poverty, inequality or unemployment.

Underdevelopment of the Third World was seen as a consequence of development of the colonial West. In other words, it was an outcome of the ruthless exploitation and deprivation of the erstwhile colonies by their European colonial masters. It nailed the dominant paradigm for overemphasizing the individual as locus of change and blame and neglecting the social, structural and political barriers to development. It gave way to a feeling of hopeless despondency first in Latin America and then in the entire Third World in the late 1960s and through the 1970s. It was realized that the mainstream modernization discourse on development had failed to deliver. This led to the demand to replace the growth-led models of development where the social and ecological dimensions were mere add-ons.

The developing countries tried hard to achieve

independent economic growth outside the world market system. For this purpose, they made concerted efforts in the United Nations for altering the rules of the game in the economic field and began to press for a New International Economic Order or NIEO. The new order was meant to ensure better representation in international economic institutions, a fairer trading system, the regulation of foreign investment, autonomy in economic matters, more economic aid, and reforms to ensure a more stable and equitable financial and monetary system.

As a result, in 1974, the UN General Assembly approved the demand for the creation of a New International Economic Order (NIEO), a democratic independent economic order, based on equality and sovereignty, including the right to 'pursue progressive social transformation that enables the full participation of the population in the development process'. [5]

2.3.1 The NWICO Debate: At the same time, demand was also raised to link the new economic order to a New World Information and Communication Order (NWICO). The proponents of NWICO held the existing international information system responsible for perpetuating and strengthening inequality in development. This had serious implications for the countries of the South which were heavily dependent on the North for both software and hardware in the information sector. The Third World leaders strongly contended that through their control of major international information channels and in the name of 'free flow' of information, the Western media was giving an exploitative and distorted view of their countries to the rest of the world.

It was argued that there existed a 'flagrant quantitative imbalance' between North and South created by the volume of news and information emanating from the developed world and intended for the developing countries and the volume of flow in the opposite direction'. "By transmitting to developing countries only news processed by them, that is news which they have filtered, cut and distorted, the transnational media imposed their own way of seeing the world upon the developing countries'. [6] As a result, the existing order had created a model of dependence with negative effects on the polity, economy and society of developing countries. The list of complaints, articulated by Tunisian Information Minister Mustapha Masmoudi, had the following points:

1. Owing to the socio-technological imbalance there was a one-way flow of information from the 'centre' to the 'periphery', which created a wide gap between the 'haves' and the 'have nots';
2. The information rich were in a position to dictate terms to the information poor, thus creating a structure of dependency with widespread economic, political and social ramifications for the poor societies;
3. This vertical flow (as opposed to a desirable horizontal flow of global information) was dominated by the Western-based transnational corporations;
4. Information was treated by the transnational media as a 'commodity' and subjected to the rules of the market;
5. The entire information and communication order was a part of and in turn propped up international inequality that created and sustained mechanisms of neo-colonialism. [7]

The demands and proposals for NWICO emerged from a series of meetings of the Non-Aligned Movement, particularly in Algiers in 1973 and Tunis in 1976. The 1975 Helsinki Conference on Security and Cooperation in Europe (CSCE) encouraged the non-aligned countries to demand these changes in global economic and information systems. The conference recognized the need for 'freer and wider dissemination of information of all kinds'. [8] Juan Somavia, a Chilean scholar, observed: "It is becoming increasingly clear that the transnational communications system has developed with the support and service of the power structure. It is an integral part of the system which affords the control of that key instrument of contemporary society viz. information. It is the vehicle of transmitting values and lifestyles to Third World countries which stimulate the type of consumption and the type of society necessary to the transnational system as a whole". [9]

A landmark in these efforts was reached with the Mass Media Declaration by UNESCO General Assembly in 1978, which recognized the role the mass media played in development. Later in December of that year, the 33rd session of the United Nations General Assembly adopted a resolution on the New World Information and Communication Order (NWICO). With the adoption of NWICO, development emerged as an integral, value-loaded, cultural process that took in natural environment, social relations, education, production, consumption and welfare. [10]

However, critics of NWICO saw in it a 'Soviet-inspired' Third World design to control the mass media through state regulation. They argued that NWICO with its 'cultural self-determination' was a mere pretext to stifle media freedom, to impose censorship and keep away foreign journalists as had happened in India and other non-aligned countries. And, they were not wrong. For instance, India's pro-Soviet authoritarian Prime Minister Indira Gandhi, not only rigged the general elections of 1971 [11] but also imposed Emergency on the intervening night of June 24-25, 1975, during which the entire non-left opposition was put behind bars and press censorship was clamped on the Indian media. The author's father too was jailed for 19 months and, in the first few weeks of his incarceration in Delhi's maximum security Tihar Jail, he had lost seven kilograms of body weight due to poor quality of food served to the inmates. The ensuing weakness made him so sick and it was even difficult for him to stand for a few minutes to meet his family—wife and two daughters. In fact, another book may be needed to share the horrifying experiences of Emergency in India.

2.3.2 The MacBride Commission: The NWICO was followed by the setting up of the International Commission for the Study of Communication Problems in 1979. The MacBride Commission, as it was popularly known, submitted its final report to the UNESCO in 1980. The report was a document which, for the first time, brought information and communication-related issues, on the global agenda.

Considering the importance of mass media in meeting the development objectives, the 16-member Commission, chaired by Sean MacBride of Ireland, was appointed to study four main aspects of global communication. They were as under:

1. The current state of world communication.
2. The problems surrounding a free and balanced flow of information and how the needs of the developing countries link with the flow.
3. How, in the light of the NIEO, a NWICO could be created.
4. How the media could become the vehicle for educating public opinion about world problems.

In its final report, the Commission laid stress on democratization of communication. It agreed that democratization was impeded by undemocratic political systems, bureaucratic administrative systems, technologies controlled or understood only be a few, the exclusion of disadvantaged groups, and illiteracy and semi-literacy. To break these barriers, it recommended participation in media management by representatives of the public and various citizens groups, horizontal communication, counter-information and three forms of alternative communication: radical opposition, community or local media movements and trade unions or other social groups with their particular communication networks.

The report of the McBride Commission was submitted to UNESCO at its 21st General Conference Session held in Belgrade in 1980 where a resolution for the attainment of a NWICO was passed. The resolution proposed the following:

1. Elimination of the imbalance and inequalities which characterize the present situation.
2. Elimination of the negative effects of certain monopolists, public or private, and excessive concentrations.
3. Removal of the internal and external obstacles to a free flow and wider and better balanced dissemination of

information and ideas.

4. Plurality of sources and channels of information.
5. Freedom of the press and information.
6. Freedom of journalists and all professionals in the communication media, a freedom inseparable from responsibility.
7. The capacity of developing countries to achieve improvement of their own situations, notably by providing their own equipment, by training their personnel, by improving their infrastructures and by making their information and communication media suitable to their needs and aspirations.
8. The sincere will of developed countries to help them attain these objectives.
9. Respect for each people's cultural identity and for the rights of each nation to inform the world public about its interests, its aspirations and its social and cultural values.
10. Respect for the right of all people to participate in international exchange of information on the basis of equality, justice and mutual benefit.
11. Respect for the right of the public, of ethnic and social groups and of individuals to have access to information sources and to participate actively in communication process. [12]

2.3.3 Right to Communicate: Following the UNESCO definition of 'a free flow and wider and more balanced dissemination of information', the McBride Report related freedom of the press to freedom of speech and expression, to the rights to communicate and receive information, rights of reply and correction, and the civil political economic-social-cultural rights set forth in the United Nation's 1966 covenants. The report pointed out that the freedom for a 'strong' and the 'haves' have had negative undesirable consequences for the 'weak' and the 'have nots'. It called for abolition of 'censorship or arbitrary control of information' asking for 'self-censorship' by communicators themselves'.

This had positive ramifications. The decade of the 1980s saw greater focus on participatory decision-making and knowledge-sharing on a co-equal basis between senders and receivers. Gender issue gained prominence with research into investigating gender gaps and ways to close them from dominating the development scenario.

However, an important development of this decade was that though the dominant paradigm of development through modernization was discarded by communication and development scholars, it never really passed off. The national governments, the power blocs and the transnationals continued to practice and propagate it. The national governments kept trying to catch up with the advanced industrialized countries in matter of new technology and modern approaches. This was particularly evident in the area of rural development with the help of telecommunications.

Telecommunications entered the field of development communications in the early 1980s and included broadcast media and the telephone as well as related technologies such as teleconferencing, audio conferencing and satellite communications. As a result, several rural communications projects that established linkages between telephony and rural development were launched in Alaska, India, Indonesia and the South Pacific. Some of the assumptions of the Maitland Commission Report on the Worldwide Telecommunications Development were as follows:

1. Telecommunication use benefits the society and the economy;
2. Improves cost-benefits of rural social service delivery;
3. Improves cost-benefits for rural economic activities; and
4. Permits more equitable distribution of economic benefits; facilitates social change and improves quality of life. [13]

2.4 Sustainability Turn

Meanwhile, the growing chorus to reconcile economic development with environmental protection resulted in a 'sustainability turn' during the 1980s. At the heart of this shift were the pressing issues like poverty reduction and climate change. The publication of the Brundtland Report in 1987 brought the concept of sustainable development to the centre of global development discourse. This concept of development integrated economic, social and environmental objectives by stressing: "...the 'environment' is where we live; and 'development' is what we all do in attempting to improve our lot within that abode. The two are inseparable".

The report defined "sustainable development as the development that meets the needs of the present without compromising the ability of the future generations to meet their own needs. This definition hinges on two key concepts: first, is the concept of 'needs', in particular the essential needs of the world's poor, to which overriding priority should be given; and second, the idea of limitations imposed by the state of technology and social organization on the environment's ability to meet present and future needs".

The basic premise of sustainable development approach is the intergenerational equity characterized by interdependent freedoms and choices i.e. the freedoms of future generations in relation to the freedoms of the present generation. The 2011 Human Development Report defined sustainable development as "the expansion of the substantive freedoms of people today while making reasonable efforts to avoid seriously compromising on those of future generations". This broadly reflects the concept of universalism that argues that the life experiences of all individuals within and across generations are equally important. Thus, sustainability is a matter of distributional equity both within and across generations.

In its report entitled "Our Common Future', the Brundtland Commission, formally known as the World Commission on Environment and Development (WECD), insisted that development was not just about how poor countries can ameliorate their situation, but what the entire world, including developed countries, can do to ameliorate our common situation. Thus, by integrating economic growth, environmental protection and social equality in the concept of sustainable development, the Commission took the global development discourse to an altogether different level.

In what is seen as an indictment of the affluent North for neglecting the world's poor, the Commission, chaired by former Norwegian Prime Minister, Gro Harlem Brundtland, said: "Development issues must be seen as crucial by the political leaders who feel that their countries have reached a plateau towards which other nations must strive. Many of the development paths of the industrialized nations are clearly unsustainable. And the development decisions of these countries, because of their great economic and political power, will have a profound effect upon the ability of all people to sustain human progress for generations to come".

Similarly, it expressed serious concerns over how the uncontrolled population in the South was putting enormous demographic pressure on the ecosystem. It said: "The question of population—of population pressure, of population and human rights—and the links between these related issues and poverty, environment, and development proved to be one of the more difficult concerns with which we had to struggle. The differences of persp ctives seemed at the outset to be unbridgeable, and they required a lot of thought and willingness to communicate across the divides of cultures, religions, and regions".

It further said: "Many critical survival issues are related to uneven development, poverty and population growth. They all place unprecedented pressures on the planet's land, water, forests, and other natural resources. The downward spiral of poverty and environmental degradation is a waste of opportunities and resources. In particular, it is a waste of human resources. These links between poverty, inequality and environmental degradation, formed a major theme in our analysis and recommendations. What is needed now is a new era of economic growth—growth that is forceful and at the same time socially and environmentally sustainable".

Calling for major changes to realize the objective of sustainable development, the Commission observed: Tragedies such as the African famines, the leak at the pesticide factory (Union Carbide) in Bhopal, India, and the nuclear disaster at Chernobyl, the USSR, appeared to justify the grave predictions about the human future that were becoming commonplace during the mid-1980s. But at public hearings that we held on five continents, we also heard from the individual victims of more chronic, widespread disasters: the debt crisis, stagnating aid to and investment in developing countries, falling commodity prices and falling personal incomes. We became convinced that major changes were needed, both in attitudes and in the way our societies are organized".

Focusing its attention on various areas of concern such as population, food security, the loss of species and genetic resources, energy, industry, and human settlements, the Commission said that all of them were connected and cannot be treated in isolation from each other. This led to Agenda 21, a non-binding voluntary implementation action plan of the United Nations with regards to sustainable development.

2.5 Human Development Approach

The end of the Cold War and the disintegration of the Soviet Union profoundly impacted the contours of development discourse. The demise of communism was hailed as a triumph of liberal democracy and capitalist free market. Words such as 'glasnost' (openness) and 'perestroika' (restructuring) not only indicated a fundamental shift in Moscow's thinking, but also became an integral part of global consciousness. This got amply reflected in UNDP's first Human Development Report of 1990 which, for the first time, took an inclusive view of development and acknowledged that the basic objective of human development is to enlarge the range of people's choices to make development more human, sustainable, democratic and participatory.

In a way, the Report not only acknowledged but also reiterated what the pioneering developmental economist Arthur Lewis had said way back in 1955 that the 'appropriate' objective of development is increasing 'the range of human choice' while adding that 'the growth of output per head gives man greater control over his environment and thereby increases his freedom'.

"These choices", it said, "should include access to income and employment opportunities, education and health, and a clean and safe physical environment. Each individual should also have the opportunity to participate fully in community decisions and to enjoy and keep changing according to circumstances and aspirations".

Later, both Dreze and Sen further elaborated Lewis's basic premise and said: "One way of seeing development is in terms of the expansion of the real freedoms that the citizens enjoy to pursue the objectives they have reason to value, and in this sense, the expansion of human capability can be, broadly, seen as the central feature of the process of development". [14]

Rejecting the one-dimensional approach to development, the Report said: "People's priorities are not fixed forever. They change over time as circumstances and aspirations change. And they must all be taken together—with no single dimension pursued at the expense of any other. Many policy makers frequently concentrate on just one dimension—income. But this concentration is at best an oversimplification and at worst a gross distortion of reality.

Underlining the basic objective of development as the expansion of human capabilities, it said: "Men, women and children must be the centre of attention—with development woven around people, not people around development. Moreover, development must be participatory, and for this, people must have the opportunity to invest in development of their capabilities—in their health, education and training. They must also have the opportunity to put their capabilities to use—to be fully involved in all aspects of life, to express themselves freely and creatively", it said.

Linking economic growth to human development, it said, human development requires economic growth—for without it, no sustained improvement in human well-being is possible. But while growth is necessary for human development, it is not enough. High growth rates do not automatically translate into higher levels of human development. And firm policy action is required to forge a closer link between economic growth and human development.

"Just as economic growth is necessary for human development, human development is critical to economic growth. This two-way link must be at the heart of any enlightened policy action", the Report stressed.

The Report viewed human development as a unifying concern for both the developing and the industrial countries. "So too is the question of development's sustainability. Each generation must meet today's needs without incurring debts it cannot repay: financial debts, by over borrowing; social debts, by neglecting to invest in people; demographic debts, by allowing unchecked population growth; and environmental debts, by exhausting natural resources".

As regards sustainable development, the human development approach goes way beyond protection and conservation of natural resources and the environment. It holds that environmental degradation exerts larger, unequal impacts on poor, marginalized and vulnerable people; and that climate change affects the people and countries the most that have least contributed to it.

The Report also introduced the human development index (HDI)—a more realistic statistical measure of development than mere gross national product (GNP) per head. The HDI merged income with life expectancy and literacy to give an overall figure and ranking. Subsequently, its scope was further widened to include the inequality-adjusted human development index (IHDI), the gender development index (GII) and the multidimensional poverty index (MPI) to quantify the scale of human deprivations globally. It thus set the agenda for human development in the 1990s which, inadvertently, coincided with the onset of globalization.

2.6 Globalization: A Mixed Baggage

The end of Cold War coincided with the arrival of globalization on the bandwagon of information and communication technologies (ICTs) in the 1990s. It characterized the dawn of a new world order in which the public ownership of state assets model including state-controlled media organisations, represented in its extreme form in the Soviet system, was dismantled. Privatization became the order of the day with the opening of new markets in Eastern Europe and the former USSR. Hailed as an engine of growth, globalization had tremendous implications for developing societies.

Most of the developing countries, including India, that were foolishly committed to the socialist model of economic planning, turned towards free market capitalist economy and welcomed foreign investors. The growth opportunities thus created enabled many of them to progress from slow-moving economies to fast-moving economies. Of these, the four biggest emerging economies—Brazil, Russia, India and China (BRICS) accounted for two-fifths of the global GDP growth in 2007. Many others like Ireland, Mexico, Venezuela, Thailand, Malaysia, Indonesia, the Philippines, South Africa and Turkey come in the category of emergent economies.

Globalization has led to off-shoring or trans-nationalization of production with maximum output and minimum input. Off-shoring involves breaking down of the production process into several parts and allocating them to different production sites around the world with a view to subsequently integrate them into a final product in one or more places. This helps in cutting costs by availing cheap labour, lower taxes and subsidized electricity, water, etc. in developing countries. It also helps in jumping tariff walls to capture foreign markets. China emerged as a powerhouse of low-cost manufacturing through off-shoring although the poor quality of goods produced there has brought it a bad name. India too launched its 'Make in India' initiative which was redefined as "Make with India" by Israeli Prime Minister Benjamin Netanyahu during Prime Minister Narendra Modi's visit to the Jewish state in July 2017.

Outsourcing of services is another defining feature of globalization. The boom in ICTs has enabled multinational companies in the United States and other developed countries to outsource services like customer care, medical transcription, and call centres around the world. The world's major corporations, from banking to insurance, and pharmaceuticals to engineering and accounting, send work offshore. This has made India a hub of outsourcing. Today, millions of young, qualified, English speaking Indians are employed in the business process outsourcing or BPO sector. Globalization has thus created jobs and opportunities for higher income for millions of people around the world. According to an estimate, 453 million people—190 million of them women—were working in global value chains in 2013, up from 296 million in 1995.

Likewise, global trade in merchandise and services amounted to almost US$24 trillion in 2014, up from US$13 trillion in 2005. Similarly, knowledge-intensive flows increased 1.3 times faster than labour-intensive flows, thanks to technological revolution, particularly the digital revolution, that has resulted in increasing interconnectedness. Globalization has thus led to growing recognition of the worldwide human commonality; as the ultimate expression of capitalism, where "the market" alone determines the restructuring of economic, political and cultural life; and also as the reorganization of networks and institutions across global space.

Another major outcome of globalization is the de-coupling of economies i.e. economic activity in emerging economies is decoupling from that of the developed world. This has speeded up growth in emerging economies that have gained by an increase in domestic demand and trade with each other. Together with off-shoring of production and outsourcing of services, decoupling has become an area of concern for developed countries. For instance, the profits of US companies like Coca Cola, IBM and DuPont in the year 2008 and onwards were better than expected due to sharp growth in sales in emerging markets which offset an equally sharp slowdown in sales in the US. Similarly, off-shoring of manufacturing and outsourcing of services not only cut jobs in the US but also in Australia where unemployment soared. The resultant frustration and discontent among disgruntled youth often got manifested in anti-racist attacks on Asians, particularly the Indians.

This gave way to renewed demand for protectionism to safeguard the American interests. In fact, the 2016 US Presidential election was fought on the question of economic policy. President Trump, in an economic policy speech in Michigan arguing for the need to resurrect American manufacturing, called for a "new economic model—the American model". In his many speeches, he often recalled the economic nationalism of past presidents such as Abraham Lincoln saying: "Our great Presidents, from Washington to Jefferson to Jackson to Lincoln, all understood that a great nation must protect its manufacturing, must protect itself from the outside...". [15]

All these issues have made opinion about globalization sharply divided among experts and activists. They tend to take one of the three positions: first, there are staunch advocates of globalization; second, there are those who support globalization with some reservations; and finally, there are staunch critics of globalization.

To the proponents of globalization, it is a powerful engine of growth that has enabled developing countries like India and China to achieve rapid and sustained growth and to raise prosperity level. They argue that the fast growing economies in the era of globalization are developing countries that are aggressively integrating with the world economy. This view is endorsed by a World Bank study that shows that poverty had indeed declined sharply in some poor and populous Asian countries such as China, India, Indonesia and Vietnam. Between 1981 and 2001, the percentage of people living on less than a dollar a day decreased from 79 to 27 percent in China; from 63 to 42 percent in India and from 55 to 11 percent in Indonesia. It is also argued that the rising tide of globalization will lift all boats, i.e. all people will gain in the long-run.

For instance, in developing countries, presence of multinationals that pay higher wages and impose higher standards of efficiency, induce workers to improve their skills leading to long-term benefits. The skill enhancement drive in countries like India is a part of this process. The socio-economic benefits of globalization go way beyond. Economic growth and diversification not only foster political stability but also ensure gender equality by accelerating absorption of women into the modern economy. Furthermore, liberalization of capital mobility stimulates foreign investment and thus enables a country to grow economically.

Since globalization cannot be rolled back, the challenge is to make it more equitable in its impact. According to critics like Amartya Sen, "the central issue of contention is not the globalization itself, nor is it the use of the market as an institution, but the inequality in the overall balance of institutional arrangements—which produces very unequal sharing of the benefits of globalization. The question is not just whether the poor, too, gain something from globalization, but whether they get a fair share and a fair opportunity". [16] Similarly, Joseph Stiglitz, who worked as a chief economist at the World Bank, argues that globalization of international finance is suffering from 'global governance without global government' and that it is necessary to change this condition and the WTO and the IMF should operate with increased transparency. [17] He has criticized the IMF for designing policies that help international lenders but adversely affect firms and workers in the developing world.

According to a survey, during 1981-2001, the proportion of Africans living below a dollar a day had increased from 42 to 47 percent. But this may not be the result of lack of opening their economies to world forces but of factors such as bad governance, political unrest, poor education system and climate change. Others, however, believe that the number of very poor people is falling fast. They see globalization as a means to promote economic growth and gain access to goods and services aspired. It is estimated that the real incomes of the poorest 20 percent rose by 4 percent in Asia and 2 percent in Africa between 1990 and 2007.

However, to the staunch critics, globalization should at best be rolled back as the business across nations has increased but has not lessened disparities between the rich and poor countries as well as between the rich and poor people within each country. For instance, sub-Saharan Africa became the poster-child of failed globalization. According to UNDP survey, [18] this region ranks the lowest amongst all geographical regions in terms of human development with a human development index of 0.5 for the year 2000. 30 out of 34 countries at the bottom of the index are in sub-Saharan Africa.

Over the years, resentment with perceived negative outcomes of globalization, has given way to a strong anti-globalization movement against it. The votaries of this global grassroots movement do not condemn the network of linkages that today encircles the world. They also appreciate the growing efficiency of markets. What they strongly oppose is the unbridled capitalism with its political and economic infrastructure that has eaten away small domestic enterprises and rendered people jobless. For instance, in India, the 'Swadeshi' movement with its stress on khadi and other domestic produce led by Pantanjali, symbolizes this overwhelming public sentiment in favour of local goods in local markets.

However, the anti-globalization movement itself has been a subject of criticism. Led by a disparate group of anti-capitalists, leftists, environmentalists, labour unions, pro-bio-diversity or just plain anti-Americans, the movement lacks any coherent goal despite talk of alternative visions, strategies and techniques. This was clear when protesters, a medley crowd of trade unions and environmentalists, gathered outside the venue of the Third Ministerial Conference of the World Trade Organization at Seattle from November 30 to December 3, 1999. The US textile and clothing trade unions were protesting against the use of child labour to shut down imports from the developing world. They were, in fact, protesting against freer trade as it ostensibly pitted US jobs against cheaper imports from the developing countries.

The environmentalists were concerned that freer trade would only benefit the multinationals which, in their greed for profits, would not only modify food products to endanger human health but also relocate to countries with inadequate safety standards. This would endanger the entire ecosystem—from rainforests to dolphins, sea turtles and butterflies. Then there were those who feared that WTO governance of trade was diluting national sovereignty, worsening employment and adding to poverty in the Third World. They were apprehensive that the Quad countries—the US, Canada, the EU and Japan—would turn the contending issues of labour standards and environment into protectionist levers to further widen the gulf between the North and the South.

Similarly, damaging effects of globalization through exploitative economic practices could be seen in dumping, that emerged as another contentious issue in world trade. Dumping is defined as a situation in which the export price of a product is lower than its selling price in the exporting country. A product is said to have been dumped if it is introduced into the commerce of another country at less than the normal value of the product and it causes or threatens material injury to an established industry of the country. Article VI of the GATT stipulates that 'in order to offset or prevent dumping, a contracting party may levy on any dumped product an antidumping duty not greater in amount than the margin of dumping in respect of such countries'. [19] As a result, all WTO member countries have either adopted or amended their anti-dumping legislation largely in accordance with the GATT provisions to deal with dumped imports. The fact that anti-dumping measures are an exception to the rule of the most-favoured nation (MFN) treatment, their invocation necessitates utmost care.

However, unlike safeguard measures, which are also instrumental for the protection of domestic industry, the implementation of anti-dumping measures does not require the government to provide offsetting concessions or consent to countermeasures taken by the trading partner. This has led to the abuse of anti-dumping measures. Therefore, countries adversely affected by them are compelled to initiate litigation for fair trade practices. India, for instance, is currently pursuing eight anti-dumping cases, of which, seven are against China.

These include: Ofloxacin originating in or exported from China PR; O-Acid originating in or exported from China PR; Textured tempered glass whether coated or uncoated from China PR; Colour coated pre-painted flat products alloy non-alloy steel from China PR; Sewing machine needle originating in or exported from China PR; Wire rod of alloy or non-alloy steel originating in or exported from China PR; Amoxycillin originating in or exported from China PR; and, Flexible slabstock polygol originating from Thailand. [20]

In short, it would be appropriate to say that globalization has integrated people, markets and work through digital revolution, yet it has done little to change the uneven human development. Contrary to expectations, progress has bypassed groups, communities and societies in such a way that people have been left out here, there, everywhere. Some of them have achieved only the basics of human development, and some not even that. Human deprivations in the form of multidimensional poverty persist everywhere. Millions of people around the world are exposed to climate-related natural disasters, droughts and associated food insecurities, subsisting on degraded land.

2.7 Millennium Development Goals

By the turn of the millennium, concerns about increasing risks and vulnerability regarding globalization and liberalization, made governments and international organization to pay more attention to social development. The prevailing situation necessitated gearing the social dimensions of their development policies towards promoting inclusive and sustainable patterns of development.

The resultant social turn—a combination of shifts in ideas and policies on social issues in development agendas since the World Summit for Social Development in Copenhagen in 1995—is a growing recognition of the need to eradicate poverty, reduce inequality and protect people from the social consequences of market fundamentalism.

In a way, it is a critique of the trickle-down assumptions that link liberalization to a virtuous cycle of growth, employment generation and poverty reduction, and of the notion that the key social function of governments should be restricted to the provision of safety nets. [21]

Although privatization, liberalization and deregulation remained the order of the day, these core neo-liberal policies were now undertaken in tandem with measures that addressed the issues of poverty, corruption and lack of transparency. In short, concerns about poverty gave rise to the social turn since the 1990s and the focus shifted to social dimensions of development through 'good governance'.

Highlighting these concerns, UNDP in its report said: "Globalization has not delivered the expected shared prosperity. Unskilled workers lost jobs in many economies, and manufacturing jobs disappeared. Productivity may have increased, but this did not always translate into higher wages, and the inequality in pay between unskilled and highly skilled labour has widened considerably".

"People have struggled during the process of globalization. Those who have recently crossed the poverty line in developing countries face vulnerable employment and the traditional-middle class in high-income countries faces stagnant wages and reductions in social services. This pattern is shaping social attitudes towards globalization.

People self-defined as part of the lower middle class and working class feel less encouraged by the concept of global citizenship. The causes are invisible in indicators such as overall GDP growth or progress out of poverty by extremely poor people, yet the frustration can create political and institutional instability if left unaddressed". [22]

All this led to the Millennium Development Goals or MDGs, adopted in September 2000 by 189 countries, to reduce poverty and facilitate human development. Developed in consultation with the developing countries, the eight millennium development goals were meant to address the most pressing problems facing the Third World. These goals were as given in Table 2.1.

Almost all international funding agencies like the World Bank, the international Monetary Fund (IMF), the Organization for Economic Cooperation and Development (OECD) and the World Trade Organization (WTO) collectively committed to develop the Millennium Declaration for poverty eradication.

The MDG assigned specific responsibilities to affluent countries including increased aid, removal of trade and investment barriers, and eliminating sustainable debts of the poorest of the poor nations.

2.8 Beyond the Basics: The SDGs and the 2030 Agenda

A general review of the development discourse so far has revealed that while fulfilling basic needs is an essential part of expanding capabilities, it is insufficient to enable people to reach their full potential.

Table 2.1: Millennium Development Goals and Targets for 2015

Goals	Targets
1. Eradicate extreme poverty and hunger	* Reduce by half the proportion of people living on less than US$ 1 a day * Reduce by half the proportion of people who suffer from hunger.
2. Achieve universal primary education	* Ensure that all boys and girls complete a full course of primary schooling
3. Promote gender equality and empower women	* Eliminate gender disparity in primary and secondary education, preferably by 2005, and at all levels by 2015.
4. Reduce child Mortality	* Reduce by two-third the mortality rate among children under 5.
5. Improve maternal Health	* Reduce by three-quarters the maternal mortality ratio
6. Combat HIV/AIDS, malaria, and other diseases	* Halt and begin to reverse the spread of HIV/AIDS
7. Ensure environmental sustainability programmes	* Integrate the principles of sustainable development into country policies and programmes; Reverse loss of environmental resources. * Reduce by half the proportion of people without sustainable access to safe drinking water *Achieve significant improvement in lives of at least 100 million slum-dwellers by 2020.
8. Develop a global partnership for development	* Develop further an open, rule-based predictable, non-discriminatory trading and financial system: Include a commitment to good governance, development and poverty reduction – both nationally and internationally * Address the special needs o. the least developed countries; include tariff and quota free access for least developed countries' exports; Enhanced programme of debt relief for heavily indebted poor countries (HIPC) and cancellation of official bilateral debt; and more generous official development assistance (ODA) for countries committed to poverty reduction * Address the special needs of land locked countries and small island developing states * Deal comprehensively with the debt problems of developing countries through national and international measures in order to make debt sustainable in the long-term * In cooperation with developing countries, develop and implement strategies for productive work for youth * In cooperation with pharmaceutical companies, provide access to affordable essential drugs in developing countries * In cooperation with private sector, make available benefits of new technologies.

This view has been reinforced by various opinion polls and surveys based on subjective evaluations to suggest strong links between the surroundings and the development priorities of the individuals.

For instance, according to the 'My World Global Survey' conducted by the United Nations to assess development issues that matter most to the people, over nine million respondents have prioritized action issues from 16 options, ranging from securing good education and ensuring political freedom to tackling climate change. The top three priorities are good education, better healthcare and better job opportunities.

Similarly, a survey by the Pew Research Centre reveals that some 83 percent of respondents in 34 developing countries considered crime to be the biggest problem in their country. Other major problems were corruption, lack of healthcare, poor schools and water pollution. Likewise, income too is a major determinant of people's priorities. For instance, respondents in a nationwide opinion survey were asked about the most important factor for a happy life. The answers varied according to the income levels of the respondents. Respondents in the highest income quintile mostly cited the achievement of goals and targets, whereas respondents in the lowest income quintile cited a peaceful life without much disruption. Leading a meaningful life and enjoying the good things in life was less of a priority among respondents in the lowest income quintile, says UNDP.

Thus, people's priorities and values tend to be context-specific and depend on degree of deprivations. Both deprivation and disadvantage are invariably linked to exclusion, either intentional or unintentional, from the opportunities of one group by another group. This exclusion is probably the most potent barrier to universalism in terms of access to healthcare, education and livelihoods as well as other dimensions of well-being such as security, freedom of participation in political life and access to advanced, high-quality services.

In the context of these aspirations, it became crucial to

achieve universal human development through Sustainable Development Goals (SDGs) that followed the Millennium Development Goals (MDGs). Here, it is worthwhile to recall that the concept of sustainable development is not new. In fact, it goes back to the 1972 Only One Earth Summit in Stockholm, the 1992 Earth Summit in Rio de Janeiro and the Rio+20 Conference in 2012.

Unlike SDGs, the MDGs focused primarily on the social agenda and raised the visibility of poverty and social development as global political concerns. They did succeed in mobilizing efforts around poverty reduction and social development. Yet, they failed as they lacked a clear approach to tackle the root causes of unsustainable development. This was amply reflected in gaps and shortcomings in measures to address inequality, in particular, with regard to gender equality, economic development and productivity and employment issues. Moreover, progress in and between countries [23] was uneven and poverty and other development challenges persisted.

As a result, the international community decided to forge a universal agenda that will "leave no one behind" on the path of sustainable human development. Entitled "Transforming our World", the 2030 Agenda for Sustainable Development, launched in September 2015, aims at transforming the world by breaking the vicious circle of poverty, inequality and environmental destruction confronting people and the planet. It intends to do this by focusing on "transformational changes that require attacking the root causes that generate and reproduce the social, economic, political and environmental problems and inequities, not merely their symptoms". [24] The resultant "eco-social" turn could lead to policy integration towards greater consideration of ecological and social objectives in development strategies. This transformative '2030 Agenda' will thus guide development policy and practice at national, regional and global levels for the coming 15 years.

2.9 Sustainable Development Goals

1. End poverty in all its forms everywhere.
2. End hunger, achieve food security and improved nutrition and promote sustainable agriculture.
3. Ensure healthy lives and promote well-being for all at all ages.
4. Ensure inclusive and equitable quality education and promote lifelong learning opportunities for all.
5. Achieve gender equality and empower all women and girls.
6. Ensure availability and sustainable management of water and sanitation for all.
7. Ensure access to affordable, reliable, sustainable and modern energy for all.
8. Promote sustained, inclusive and sustainable economic growth, full and productive employment and decent work for all.
9. Built resilient infrastructure, promote inclusive and sustainable industrialization and foster innovation.
10. Reduce inequality within and among countries.
11. Make cities and human settlements inclusive, safe, resilient and sustainable.
12. Ensure sustainable consumption and production patterns.
13. Take urgent action to combat climate change and its impacts.
14. Conserve and sustainably use the oceans, seas and marine resources for sustainable development.
15. Protect, restore and promote sustainable use of terrestrial ecosystems, sustainably manage forests, combat desertification, and halt and reverse land degradation and halt biodiversity loss.
16. Promote peaceful and inclusive societies for sustainable development, provide access to justice for all and build effective, accountable and inclusive institutions at all levels.
17. Strengthen the means of implementation and revitalize the Global Partnership for Sustainable Development.

Thus, the integrated vision of the '2030 Agenda' goes beyond all previous developmental approaches discussed so far to 'rebalance' poverty reduction and social goals with economic and environmental objectives. This holistic approach to sustainable development emphasizes integration of economic and social policy while enhancing human rights, gender equality and environmental sustainability. Seen from this perspective, all countries of the world are considered 'developing'.

According to Dr. Angela Merkel, the Chancellor of the Federal Republic of Germany, the Sustainable Development Goals reflect shared vision and collective responsibilities. She says: "Human dignity is inviolable. This principle has not changed since 1948 when it was formulated by the United Nations in the Universal Declaration of Human Rights. It does not stop at national borders and applies to everyone regardless of age, gender or religion. However, up to what extent have we lived up to this high principle? How far have we progressed in reality towards ensuring that every individual can lead a life in dignity? The Human Development Report sheds light on this regularly. By placing the focus on individuals, it also highlights the necessity of investing in people, in health, in education and training, in economic and social infrastructure.

"Poverty and hunger, state fragility and terror—we are aware of these and other existential challenges. However, we also know that good human development is possible. Even in the poorest regions there are not only natural resources, but also tremendous creativity, innovative drive and a willingness to work hard. We have to make the most of these assets in order to seize the opportunities for a life in dignity—regardless of how difficult that might be in some cases.

"At a time of increasing globalization, life chances on the different continents are more closely interconnected than ever before. It is, therefore, all the more important to act jointly on the basis of shared values. That is why we adopted the '2030 Agenda' with its global Sustainable Development Goals. That is why we have concluded a global climate agreement. As a result of these instruments, all states have an obligation and responsibility to tackle the key challenges facing humankind—from the eradication of poverty and the protection of the climate, nature and the environment to ensuring peace.

"In many respects, viable answers to such crucial questions require us to fundamentally change how we think and act in the way we live and work. The economy, social issues and the environment have an impact on each other. Economic productivity, social responsibility and protection of the natural resources on our planet therefore have to be reconciled. This is exactly the meaning of the principle of sustainability, which the '2030 Agenda' is aiming for. In its essence, it is about nothing less than a life in dignity, justice and peace, a life in an intact environment, social security and the opportunity for every individual to reach their economic potential". [25]

Clearly, the SDGs are more holistic in approach. They address the interconnectedness of social, environmental and economic elements. They have reinstated the concept of sustainable development as the overarching framework for policy making and governance into the future. Their people-friendly and planet-sensitive approach has helped in integrating social perspective into mainstream development strategies through transformational potential of reforms and innovations.

However, implementation of the '2030 Agenda' and the SDGs is not an easy task. According to experts, the realization of its transformative potential is a huge challenge that requires different types of innovations in conceptual approaches, policies, institutions and social relations to address the root causes of poverty, hunger, inequality, climate change and unsustainable practices. "It will also require moving from declarations of intent toward implementation by designing appropriate policies and institutions, leveraging the political will and consensus as well as the financial and administrative means to implement them. It will require multiple actions from the top down and the bottom up, involving all members of the society. At each step, from innovating to integrating and implementing, the nature of the political process in terms of inclusiveness, transparency and accountability will be crucial. As much as the outcomes, the processes related to the implementation of the SDGs will be the litmus test of the very principle of universalism and human rights inherent in the 2030 Agenda". [26]

Endnotes

1. Schramm, Wilbur (1964), "Mass Media and National Development", UNESCO, Paris, p. 27.
2. Kindleberger, C.P. (1965), "Economic Development".
3. Goulet, Denis (1971), "The Cruel Choice: A New Concept in the Theory of Development", New York: Atheneum, pp. 87-94.
4. Lewis, Arthur W. (1963), "Is Economic Growth Desirable" in Allen and Unwin (eds.), 'Theory of Economic Growth', London: Harper, p. 420.
5. Hamelink, C. (1979), "Informatics: Third World Call for New Order", *Journal for Communication*, 29, 4, p. 144.
6. Masmoudi, M. (1979), "The New World Information Order", *Journal of Communication*, 29, 2, pp. 172-173.
7. Ibid.
8. Nordenstreng, K. (1986), "New International Information and Communication Order Source Book", Prague: International Organisation of Journalists.
9. Somavia, J. (1976), "The Transnational Power Structure and International Information", *Development Dialogue*, 2, pp. 16-17.
10. Kumar, Keval J. (1994), "Mass Communication in India", Bombay: Jaico.
11. Madhok, Balraj (1978), "Murder of Democracy".
12. UNESCO, 1980.
13. Maitland Commission (1984), "The Missing Link: Report of the Independent Commission for Worldwide Telecommunications Development", Geneva: ITU.
14. Dreze Jean and Amartya Sen (2005), "India: Development and Participation", New Delhi: Oxford University Press.
15. Hendrickson, John (2017), "The Roots of Trump's Economic

Policy", in themorningglory/Shutterstock.
16. Sen, Amartya (2002), "How to Judge Globalism?", *The American Prospect*, 13, 1, January, pp. 1-14.
17. Stiglitz, Joseph (2002), "Globalization and its Discontents", New Delhi: Penguin India.
18. UNDP, 2002.
19. Aggarwal, Aradhna (2002), "Anti-dumping Law and Practice: An Indian Perspective", New Delhi: ICRIER.
20. "Anti-dumping Cases in India", Department of Commerce, Ministry of Commerce and Industry, Government of India.
21. UNRISD, 2016.
22. UNDP, 2016.
23. World Bank, 2016.
24. UNRISD, 2015b.
25. Human Development Report, 2016.
26. UNRISD, 2016.

3

Theories and Paradigms of Development

As understood so far, development means different things to different people at different times. It defies any set definition. So is the broad conceptual framework of development that has been evolving since its initial formulation in the late 1940s. Yet, there are certain overarching concepts or theories that indicate various milestones in its evolutionary journey. They range from the initial modernization perspective that became the dominant paradigm of development in the 1950s and 1960s to the critical perspective or the dependency theory of the late 1960s and early 1970s and the post-modernist alternative paradigm of the 1980s with emphasis on culture and empowerment through participation. The 'liberal-social turn' to human development in the post-Cold War era paved way for the 'eco-social sustainability turn' to the 2030 Agenda in the 21st century global development discourse.

3.1 Sociology of Development

The sociology of development grew out of the evolutionary perspective on human societies. It was inspired by Charles Darwin's pet theory of 'the survival of the fittest' as given in his book, 'On the Origin of the Species, 1859'. Darwin argued that all organisms had evolved from simpler forms and that the general direction of biological evolution was unilinear that is towards more complex forms. Other theorists of this Evolutionist school included Herbert Spencer and William Sumner who further applied Darwin's ideas to the process of modernization of human societies. They compared transformation of cultures to the evolution of organisms in biological sciences. "The growth of cultures was inextricably tied, as in the growth of organisms, to a series of inevitable and irreversible stages. In these theories of social evolution, the development of societies followed a unilinear path and the major stages of growth were universal". [1] Spencer went a step further to claim the superiority of Western societies over all other races as they were adapted to face the changing conditions in the process of modernization of societies.

These theories of social evolution paved way for various bi-polar theories of modernization that reduced social evolution to 'ideal-typical' extremes or end points of the process of social transformation of the nations in Europe and North America. Some of the well-known bi-polar theories were: Maine (1907) Status vs. Contract; Durkheim (1933) Mechanic vs. Organic Solidarity; Toennies (1957) Gemeinschaft vs. Gesellschaft; Lerner (1958) Traditional vs. Modern Society; Cooley (1962) Primary vs. Secondary Social Attachments; and Redfield (1965) Folk vs. Urban Societies. [2] "Theorists in this tradition were less concerned with encompassing the entire history of mankind than with apprehending the moment of European transition from a feudal-agricultural to a capitalist-industrial order', notes Portes. [3] Based on them, the underdeveloped Third World was considered traditional while the developed West signified its modern counterpart.

3.1.1 Social Differentiation: The modern West was characterized by a wide range of systemic autonomy which means capacity, either innate or acquired, to cope with a range of social, cultural, technological and economic issues in the process of social change. The Third World, in contrast, not only lacked higher differentiation of roles and institutions, but was also constrained by its limited capacity to cope with their own problems. Thus, social differentiation, a direct outcome of the social evolutionary theories, was another key feature of the unilinear perspective on development through modernization.

According to this theory, societies modernize through greater and greater differentiation in their institutions. In simpler societies, there is hardly any differentiation in social institutions. A single institution may perform several functions. Thus, a process of differentiation takes place where several institutes take over the functions that were hitherto undifferentiated and performed by one or a couple of institutions. The process of differentiation is accompanied by the concomitant process of integration. "The theory of society based on this notion is one in which pressures faced at a given point are eliminated through increasing specialization and differentiation, which, in turn, give rise to problems of integration, which are solved through emerging networks of interdependence. The whole process results in an ever-growing societal 'complexity' or 'systemness'. [4]

3.1.2 Social Mobilization: Social differentiation was to be accompanied by social mobilization defined as "the process in which old social, economic, and psychological commitments are eroded and broken down and people become available for new patterns of socialization and behaviour". [5] A measure of this process not only included higher social differentiation and integration of roles and institutions but also the development of certain universals such as money, markets, democratic association, a common legal system and most importantly, growth of a powerful bureaucratic state on account of shift in political legitimacy from divine monarchical rule to the nation-state and sovereignty of its people. Once these key institutions and certain behavioural patterns were well entrenched, development could take place in a sustained unilinear manner. Therefore, the modern West with all its political, economic, social and cultural modernization, evolutionary universals like a wide range of systemic autonomy and features of an industrial society became a model for the Third World to emulate.

At the micro level, importance was given to change at the individual level as the key to social transformation through modernization. Therefore, theories on individual psychology, based on Weber's thesis on Protestant Ethic (1958) which was anchored within the power relationships, structural constraints, and political-economic interest in Catholic Europe, stressed attitudinal or behavioural changes as essential prerequisites of a modern society. For instance, in 1966, David McClelland in order to identify and measure the impulse of modernization separated a mental virus that made people behave in a particularly energetic way. Earlier in 1962, Everett Hagen tried to empirically determine the measure that influenced entrepreneurial activity in his concept of 'withdrawal of status respect'. Portes sums up this complex psychonalaytic variable thus: "Humiliations resulting from status withdrawal among parents have certain psychic consequences for their sons who, in turn, transmit them to their own children. After a complicated evolution of complexes and stages, the 'virus' finally matures and is ready to do its work in the society". [6]

On the other hand, Daniel Lerner (1958) in his theory of modernization talked about a 'mobile and change-accepting' personality. Mobile individuals were endowed with empathy or a capacity to identify with another. To him, empathy was the predominant personal style in Western countries which were industrial, urban, literate and participant, unlike the backward and underdeveloped Third World. He, therefore, strongly recommended development of empathy as an indispensable skill for people to move out of traditional settings and opt for modernization.

Based on his research on individual modernity in six developing countries, Alex Inkeles argued that the transformation of individuals was both a means to an end and an end in itself of the development process. He constructed an ideal modern personality with the help of nine attitudes such as: (i) readiness of new experiences and openness of innovation; (ii) disposition to form and hold opinions; (iii) democratic orientation; (iv) planning habits; (v) belief in human and personal efficacy; (vi) belief that the world is calculable; (vii) stress on personal and human dignity; (viii) faith in science and technology; and (ix) belief in distributive justice. [7]

3.1.3 Culture: The role of culture in development was also critically examined by scholars like Weber who identified a set of cultural values in Asian thought processes—its orthodox religions and quaint philosophies—that inhibited modernization. Therefore, proponents of modernization aggressively advocated extension of the modernization components and displacement of all traditional or Asian elements in developing nations. [8] This antipathy towards everything orient, be its culture, tradition, religion and philosophy, in the Western mindset was aptly summed up in 'A Passage to India by E.M. Forster as: "East is east and West is west, the twain shall never meet".

3.2 Dominant Paradigm: Modernization

The modernization approach to development was mainly concerned with economic growth as measured by the gross national product or GNP rate and encouragement of all factors and institutions that accelerated high growth rates such as capital-intensive industrialization, high technology, private ownership of production, free trade and principle of *laissez-faire*.

A product of the post-war era, the modernization paradigm of development was overshadowed by the Cold War rivalry between the two superpowers. Both tried to promote their own versions of 'modern futures' to the poverty-stricken and debt-ridden third-world. In this race towards supremacy, the modernization paradigm promoted by the United States and its Western allies, began to dominate all spheres of social life and came to be known as the 'dominant paradigm' of development.

The dominant paradigm dictated the development discourse from the 1940s to the 1960s and longer. It strongly advocated industrialization as a preferred route to economic growth. The poor Third World countries were encouraged to go for industrialization and invest in massive hydroelectric projects, steel industries, and a range of manufacturing units. They were provided with financial assistance, technical know-how and human expertise by multilateral funding agencies.

Consequently, the capital and machine-intensive techniques substituted abundantly available labour for setting up industries financed by national governments and multilateral agencies. Development thus accrued was to be measured by quantitative indicators like gross national product (GNP) rates and per capita incomes. The influence of this dominant paradigm was all pervasive with little or no room for critical scrutiny. Almost all developing nations religiously followed this concept of development that, according to Rogers, had the following essential elements namely:

1. It held economic growth through industrialization and accompanying urbanization as the key to development. It was approximately equal to passing through the Industrial Revolution (a stage which had by-passed the erstwhile colonies). It was assumed that development performance could be quantified in economic terms like GNP (gross national product), per capita income, etc;
2. The choice of technology was to be capital intensive, and labour extensive mainly imported from developed nations;
3. In order to guide and speed up the process of development, planning should be centralized and controlled by economists and bankers; and
4. Underdevelopment was mainly due to problems within the developing nations rather than in their external relationships with other countries. [9]

However, in 'socialist' India, this paradigm was a non-starter as the myopic Indian leadership lacked both vision and wisdom to reject socialism and the Soviet prescription for economic development, something it had to do decades later in early 1990s through 'economic restructuring and reforms'. As a result, the Soviet style development model got manifested in the form of centralized economic planning through New Delhi-based Planning Commission and mammoth public sector undertakings that perpetually went red. They manufactured everything from HMT wrist watches to railway locomotives and coaches. Under the quota permit system, there was no room for private initiative for production and whatever little space was available, it was curbed by rampant corruption. All this was done at the cost of agriculture which was completely neglected. The poor debt-ridden farmer was left with little choice. He was either forced to abandon his land or commit suicide—a trend which, most unfortunately, is still visible in the 21st century India.

Decrying the perpetually loss-making public sector undertakings as the 'parasite sector', noted Parliamentarian and statesman, Prof. Balraj Madhok, had said: "It should be clearly understood that State control of all means of production and distribution as advocated by the socialists in India is incompatible with democracy. Freedom of thought and expression which sustains democracy is unthinkable without freedom of living. If everyone becomes dependent on the state for his or her living, there can be no freedom of thought and no democracy. He who pays the piper calls the tune. He who will control the state apparatus will determine what people should think and say as has been the case in the Soviet Union and other communist countries. Such socialism is therefore incompatible with democracy. Therefore, any attempt to force Soviet type of socialism on the people in the name of social change must be resisted by all democrats and nationalists. Any attempt to force the pace of social change at the cost of democracy would be self-defeating". [10]

Looking back, it now appears, as if the leadership of newly independent India was hell bent on making the country poorer by repeated monumental blunders in all spheres of national life—be it economic planning, foreign affairs or national defence. One wonders, as to how, India would have fared if Sardar Vallabh Bhai Patel had become its first prime minister; if only Dr. Shyama Prasad Mookerji and Shri Lal Bahadur Shastri had lived longer or if Prof. Balraj Madhok was not betrayed by his own men.

3.3 Diffusion of Innovation and its Adoption

The dominant paradigm of development and modernization worked through diffusion of new ideas and innovations. A range of diffusion studies inundated the pro-development atmospherics in the Third World. These studies were based on the exogenous change theory that held that static societies were brought to life by outside influences, technical aid, knowledge, resources and financial assistance and (in a slightly different form) by the diffusion of ideas. [11]

The main purpose of diffusion of innovation approach was to promote social and economic change for modernization through adoption of technology and the concomitant process of industrialization. "So, the micro level investigations of the diffusion of technological innovations in agriculture, health, family planning etc. among villagers were of direct relevance to development planners and other government officials in developing countries. These research results, and the general framework of diffusion, provided both a kind of theoretical approach and an evaluation procedure for development agencies". [12]

However, extensive sociological studies of the agrarian societies of India, Nigeria and Colombia by Rogers [13] further revealed that it was not easy for the peasantry to discard its tried and tested traditional ways in favour of new and radical changes. This peculiar situation required deep and incisive understanding of the Third World peasantry that shared certain common traits that made them resistant to adoption of innovation. They were:

1. Mutual distrust in interpersonal relations: In general, peasants were suspicious, exclusive and distrustful of others in the community and non-cooperative in interpersonal relations with peers.
2. Perceived limited good: Peasants believed that all good things in life are available in limited quantities. Thus, one could improve one's position only at somebody else's expense.
3. Dependence and hostility towards government authority: Peasants had an ambivalent attitude toward government officials. On the other hand, they depended upon them for

solving many of their problems. However, there was a general distrust of government leaders.

4. Familism: The family played an important role in the life of a peasant. Peasants were prepared to subordinate their personal goals to those of the family.
5. Lack of innovativeness: Peasants were reluctant to adopt modernizing innovations, had a negative attitude towards change, and their behaviour was not fully oriented toward rational economic considerations.
6. Fatalism: Peasants believed that their well-being was controlled by a supernatural fate. This had a dysfunctional consequence on directed special change.
7. Limited aspirations: Peasants exhibited low aspirations for advancement. Also, they had low levels of achievement motivation and a tendency toward inconspicuous consumption.
8. Lack of deferred gratifications: Peasants lacked the ability to postpone satisfaction of immediate needs in anticipation of better future rewards.
9. Limited view of the world: First they were not time conscious. Second, they were localites. They were oriented within their communities and had no orientation to the (outside) world beyond their narrow group. Consequently, they had very limited geographic mobility.
10. Low empathy: Peasants exhibited mental inertness. They could not imagine themselves in new situations or places.

This behavioural profiling of the Third World peasantry, decried as laggards, was defined as 'subculture of peasantry' by Rogers. [14] This description, according to Melkote, further substantiated the 'individual blame bias' in the stereotypical analysis of traditional individual in modernization studies by scholars like Daniel Lerner, David McClelland and Everett Hagen. However, this analysis of the marginalized peasantry was later rejected by subsequent diffusion studies carried out in Kenya in 1970s that showed that resistance to adoption of innovation was not on account of the 'in-the-head variable bias' but due to non-psychological factors or bottlenecks [15] within the social, economic and political system in which the peasants were languishing. They were as under:

1. Lack of knowledge and skills about innovations to be adopted.
2. Lack of peoples' involvement in the development planning process.
3. Lack of financial and material inputs necessary for adoption.
4. Lack of inadequate market development for sale/purchase of produce.
5. Lack of infrastructure to facilitate distribution of information and material.
6. Lack of off-season employment opportunities in rural areas.

The incisive analytical study of the rural poor along with the existence of the bottlenecks necessitated 'a systematic and planned implementation' of diffusion and adoption of innovations process. To facilitate this, Rogers identified the following main elements in any analysis of diffusion or an idea or innovation. They were: (i) the innovation which is any idea considered as new by the recipient, and (ii) its communication through certain channels, (iii) among members of a social system, and (iv) overtime. [16] A similar definition was provided by Katz who defined diffusion as "the process of spread of a given new idea or practice, overtime, via specifiable channels, through a social structure such as neighbourhood, a factory, or a tribe". [17]

3.3.1 Types of Diffusion: According to Rogers, diffusion is of two types—centralized and decentralized. In a centralized diffusion system, decisions about such matters as when to begin diffusing an innovation, who should evaluate it, and through which channels it will be diffused, are made by a small number of officials and/or technical experts at the head of the change agency.

In a decentralized diffusion system, such decisions are more widely shared by the clients and potential adopters. Here, horizontal networks among the clients is the main mechanism through which innovations spread. In fact, in extremely decentralized diffusion systems, there may not be a change agency; potential adopters are solely responsible for the self-management of the diffusion of innovations. New ideas may grow out of the practical experience of certain individuals in the client system, rather than coming from the formal R&D activities.

However, until the 1970s, it was assumed that relatively centralized diffusion systems like the agriculture extension service were an essential ingredient of the diffusion process, but in recent years several relatively decentralized diffusion systems have been investigated and evaluated, and found to represent an appropriate alternative to centralized diffusion under certain conditions, says Rogers.

3.3.2 Innovation and Re-Invention: An innovation is an idea, practice, or object that is perceived as new by an individual. So far as human behaviour is concerned, it matters little, whether or not an idea is objectively new as measured by the lapse of time since its first discovery, says Rogers. The perceived newness of the idea for the individual determines his or her reaction to it. If the idea seems new to the individual, it is an innovation.

Newness in an innovation, says Rogers, need not just involve new knowledge. Someone may have known about an innovation for some time but not yet developed a favourable or unfavourable attitude towards it, nor have adopted or rejected it. The 'newness' aspect of an innovation may be expressed in terms of knowledge, persuasion, or a decision to adopt, he adds. However, characteristics of an innovation, as perceived by the individual in a social system, affect its rate of adoption. They are:

1. **Relative Advantage:** It is the degree to which an innovation is perceived as better than the idea it supersedes. The degree of relative advantage may be measured in economic terms, but social-prestige factors, convenience, and satisfaction are also often important components. It does not matter so much

whether an innovation has a great deal of objective advantage. What does matter is whether an individual perceives the innovation as advantageous. The greater the perceived relative advantage or an innovation, the most rapid its rate of adoption is going to be.

2. **Compatibility:** It is the degree to which an innovation was consistent with the existing values, past experiences, and potential adopters. An idea that is not compatible with the prevalent values and norms of a social system will not be adopted as rapidly as an innovation that is compatible. The adoption of an incompatible innovation often requires the prior adoption of a new value system. An example of an incompatible innovation is the use of contraception in countries where religious beliefs discourage the use of birth-control techniques, as in Muslim and Catholic nations.
3. **Complexity:** It is the degree to which an innovation is perceived as difficult to understand and use. Some innovations are readily understood by most members of a social system; others are more complicated and will be adopted more slowly. New ideas that are simpler to understand will be adopted more rapidly than innovations that require the adopter to develop new skills and understandings.
4. **Trialability:** It is the degree to which an innovation may be experimented with, on a limited basis. New ideas that can be tried on the instalment plan will generally be adopted more quickly than innovations that are not divisible. An innovation that is trialable represents less uncertainty to the individual who is considering it for adoption, as it is possible to learn by doing so.
5. **Observability:** It is the degree to which the results of an innovation are visible to others. The easier it is for individuals to see the results of an innovation, the more likely they are to adopt. Such visibility stimulates peer discussion of a new idea, as friends and neighbours of an adopter ask him or her for innovation-evaluation

information about it. Solar panels on a household's roof are highly observable, and a California survey found that the typical solar adopter showed his equipment to about six of his peers (Rogers et al., 1979).

3.3.3 Re-Invention: It is defined as the degree to which an innovation is changed or modified by a user in the process of adoption and implementation. According to Eveland, re-invention is also measured as the degree to which an individual's use of a new idea departs from the "mainline" version of the innovation that was initially promoted by a change agency. It has been seen that a fair degree of re-invention occurred for some innovations while other innovations are more difficult or impossible to re-invent. For instance, hybrid seed corn is virtually impossible to re-invent by a farmer as the hybrid vigour is genetically locked into first generation seed in ways that are too complicated for a farmer to change.

Thus, perception plays in important part in the adoption of an innovation and its further re-invention. Innovations that are perceived as having greater relative advantage, compatibility, trialability, observability, and less complexity will be adopted more rapidly than other innovations. "These are not the only qualities that affect adoption rates, but past research has indicated that they are the most important characteristics of innovations in explaining rate of adoption", says Rogers. [18]

3.3.4. Adoption of Innovation Process: Findings of various diffusion studies have shown that the innovation-decision process is a multi-stage process through which an individual (or other decision-making unit) passes from first knowledge of an innovation to forming an attitude towards the innovation, to a decision to adopt or reject, to implementation of a new idea, and to confirmation of this decision. It is a multi-level five stage process through which the individual arrives at or rejects the innovation from the time of getting aware about it. These five stages are:

1. Awareness or Knowledge: At this point, the recipient is

exposed to the idea and gains some understanding of how it functions but lacks detailed information about it.

2. Interest or Persuasion: At this stage, the individual is persuaded to form a favourable or unfavourable attitude towards the innovation.
3. Evaluation or Decision: Decision occurs when an individual (or other decision-making unit) engages in activities that lead to a choice to adopt or reject the innovation.
4. Trial or Implementation: Implementation takes place when an individual or the other decision-making unit puts an innovation into use. Re-invention is more likely to occur at this stage.
5. Adoption or Confirmation: Confirmation occurs when the individual or other decision-making unit seeks reinforcement of an innovation decision that has already been made. However, this decision can be reversed if exposed to conflicting messages about the innovation.

However, the multi-level innovation-decision process need not always lead to adoption, a decision to make full use of an innovation. It can also result in rejection or a decision against adopting an innovation. It can also lead to discontinuance. Discontinuance may occur on account of dissatisfaction with the innovation or its replacement with an improved idea. Either way, this decision occurs during the confirmation stage of the innovation-decision process.

While some factors stimulate and facilitate quick diffusion of innovations and transfer of technologies, factors like cultural incompatibility, perceived impact of the adoption on social relations, scope for reversibility in case the innovation is to be rejected and complexities involved in the acceptance of innovation on sustainable basis inhibit its adoption. Simple the innovation, higher is the scope for adoption, says Rogers. Of these, cultural incompatibility and resultant mismatch is considered to be very strong inhibiting factors in the process of diffusion of innovations. Many studies have substantiated that new crop varieties, which gave higher yields and better incomes, have been rejected on the ground of taste, fear of ill-health and unacceptability as food.

Research has shown that a certain degree of innovativeness is required in an individual to make a pro-adoption decision. Diffusion researchers have classified adopters into five distinct categories based on the rate of adoption and the time lag between initial exposure to final adoption. They are as under:

1. Venturesome innovators: Cosmopolitan in nature, they are enterprising and risk takers. Few in numbers, they are financially resourceful with high awareness and educational levels. They are keen to opt for a new innovation on their own volition without any external stimulus.
2. Early adopters: These are people that belong to the local system and willingly follow the venturesome innovators and are ready to change course for the better. Often they find themselves in the role of opinion leaders.
3. Early majority: They quietly follow the example set by early adopters. They repose faith in the efficacy of the new innovation with little or no reservation.
4. Late majority: These are late risers who do not want to miss the bus. Once the news or information about the innovation and its benefits percolates down, this segment tries to catch up with the latest trend in society.
5. Laggards: As the name suggests, they resent change and are slow to adopt. They are rigid and hard to be convinced, stick to old methods and resist change.

3.3.5 Role of Opinion Leaders: The role of opinion leaders as individuals who can influence peoples' decisions first came to limelight in the research conducted on the effects of mass media on the outcome of 1949 US elections. Later, Rogers in his path breaking study, 'Diffusion of Innovations', extensively dealt with the role of opinion leaders in influencing others to determine the rate of adoption of an innovation in a social system. By virtue of their hold and influence over their followers in a community or social system, the opinion leaders, who otherwise need not hold any official position, have a far greater say in matters of importance and routine affairs.

Based on their capacity to influence opinion among their peers, opinion leaders have been classified as polymorphic and monomorphic. Polymorphism is the degree to which an individual acts as an opinion leader for a variety of topics and issues. Its opposite, monomorphism, is the tendency for an individual to act as an opinion leader for only a single topic or issue. [19] However, their ability to influence a pro-innovation adoption decision is attributed to the following reasons:

1. External Communication: It is of two types. With their access to external communication via change agents and mass media channels, opinion leaders can serve as an avenue for the entrance of new ideas into their social system. Their frequent contact with change agents makes them efficient diffusion agents among their followers.
2. Accessibility: Social participation makes opinion leaders accessible to one and all. They can easily spread new ideas at formal meetings and informal discussions through face-to-face communication.
3. Socio-economic Status: According to Tarde, "invention can start from the lowest ranks of the people, but its extension depends upon the existence of some lofty social elevation". [20] It is generally seen that opinion leaders enjoy higher socio-economic status. Their privileged position primarily on account of larger land holdings and farm sizes gives them automatic recognition as competent experts about innovations. They display a marked tendency to adopt new ideas before their followers. This makes them ideal for reducing uncertainty about an innovation for their followers.

3.3.6 Role and Responsibilities of a Change Agent: During the early phase of development, the task of diffusion of innovation and its adoption was entrusted to extension workers. They were given the responsibility of information dissemination and persuasive communication for the adoption of innovation. They were selected for this task primarily because extension service was highly reputed for its logical, scientific and systematic methodology for disseminating useful knowledge and skills to the user receivers. The extension methodology was considered most suitable to decide about the best innovations for the clients and also following it up with campaigns to convince them of the wisdom of its choice. However, the original extension responsibility to collect, collate and convey all relevant research-generated information to potential clients was no longer adequate. Therefore, the information dissemination extension agent was now expected to evolve into a 'change agent or a professional person' who attempts to influence adoption decisions in a direction that he feels desirable, says Rogers. [21]

The role assigned to a change agent was to diffuse innovations to clients. Change agents provided linkage between a change agency and a client system. This led to one-way flow of influence-oriented persuasive messages from change agencies at the top to the rural peasantry at the bottom. The extension agents used face-to-face communication for the purpose.

Pro-Persuasion Model of Development [22]

Persuasive Extension Communication

↓

Adoption of Technological Innovations

↓

Individual and National Development

As professional change agents, the extension workers' role also included obtaining feedback from clients about the innovations. This was important to make the change process effective and sustainable. The overall responsibilities of an extension-cum-change agent included the following:

1. Develops need for change: Since necessity is the mother of

invention, the first responsibility of a change agent is to create a need for innovation. This begins by making the client aware of the problem/s faced by them and its relevant solution in the form of a new idea or innovation.

2. Establishes an information-exchange relationship: Since trust begets trust, clients must first accept the change agent by reposing trust in his competence only then can they accept the innovations promoted by him or her. Therefore, having identified the need, the next step for the change agent is to develop rapport with the clients. This is mainly because the innovations are often judged on the basis of how the change agent is perceived.
3. Diagnoses their problems: This is an extension of the first responsibility i.e. development of need. Here, the change agent not only analyses the problem in detail but also suggests as to why the existing alternatives do not meet the existing needs. Also, on account of his special knowledge of the innovation, a change agent can sense possible needs or problems of clients that they do not see for themselves.
4. Creates intent to change in the client: This is done by persuading and motivating the client to opt for the innovation/s in order to change. However, this desire for change must be client-centric and focus on the clients' problems rather than innovation-centric. The golden rule to remember here is that the change agent is not a salesman selling a product. Rather, he or she is a harbinger of change and development.
5. Translates intent into action: A highly motivated client opts for the innovation. This motivation can be on account of change agent's persuasive communication or inspired by near peers as well as opinion leaders.
6. Stabilizes adoption and prevents discontinuance: Since discontinuance with the innovation is a frequent occurrence, change agents can stabilize new behaviour by directing reinforcing messages to those clients who have adopted the innovation to freeze their new behaviour. This

begins at the implementation or confirmation stage in the innovation-decision process.

7. Achieves a terminal relationship: A change agent must strive to make the clients self-reliant by developing their ability to be their own change agents. This means that having adopted an innovation, the clients should cease to depend on change agents by developing a self-renewing behaviour of their own.

However, the success of a change agent is directly proportional to the degree to which the diffusion programme is compatible with clients' needs. Change programmes that are not based on clients' needs fail to deliver the desired results. To substantiate the point, Rogers cites the example of an Indian village that lacked well for drinking purposes. The women had to fetch potable water from quite a distance, approximately two miles, everyday. But the change agent somehow failed to notice this felt need of the villagers and recommended development funds only to dig a well for agricultural purposes to double the crop yield. But because the villagers were in dire need of a well for drinking purposes, the peasants dug the well in the villager centre or *chaupal*, rather than in the fields, and drank the water instead of irrigating their crops. Had the change agent paid attention to the felt needs of the villagers, he could have provided at least one well each for drinking purposes and irrigation. [23]

3.3.8 Consequences of Change Programmes: Rogers has defined consequences as the changes that occur to an individual or to a social system as a result of the adoption or rejection of an innovation. He has classified consequences as: (i) desirable versus undesirable, (ii) direct versus indirect, and (iii) anticipated versus unanticipated. The desirable consequences are the functional effects of an innovation to an individual or to a social system. Undesirable consequences are the opposite dysfunctional effects of an innovation to an individual or to a social system.

Direct consequences, says Rogers, are changes to an

individual or a social system that occur in immediate response to an innovation. Indirect consequences are the changes to an individual or a social system that occur as a result of the direct consequences of an innovation. Anticipated consequences are changes due to an innovation that are recognized and intended by the members of a social system. Unanticipated consequences are changes due to an innovation that are neither intended nor recognized by the members of a social system. Usually, the undesirable, indirect and unanticipated consequences of innovations go together as also the desirable, direct and unanticipated consequences, says Rogers.

3.4 The Passing of Dominant Paradigm

In the mid-1970s, Rogers proclaimed the 'passing' of the 'dominant paradigm' and its modernization model sans the 'diffusion of innovation' model as it had cross-cultural applications. It was based on experiences of agricultural extension studies in the United States and several developing countries including India.

However, reasons for the passing of dominant paradigm were many. Most significant was its equation of development with economic growth. The progress through growth was measured by per capita incomes or GNP. This approach did not include other indicators of economic growth such as poverty, unemployment and inequality. For instance, during the development decade of the 1960s, the rate of increase of unemployment competed with high rates of growth. [24] So was the case with inequality which increased all over the developing world. For instance, in Brazil, the top five percent cornered as much as 46 percent of the national income. Likewise, in Kenya, Ecuador and Turkey, the share of the national income was concentrated in the hands of a very small minority. While the trickle-down model encouraged some initial inequality as necessary to generate savings and incentives, the rate of inequality that actually emerged was dysfunctional to economic growth. [25]

Similarly, it had adverse impact on poverty rates as well. According to estimates, [26] as economic expansion grew, the income of the bottom 40 percent of people in developing countries fell not only relatively but in absolute terms as well. For instance, in countries like India, Brazil and Mexico, bottom half of the population had less income at the end of 1970s than they had in the early 1960s. This decline gave new fuel to the criticisms of dominant conception of mainstream development practices, which came under fire for being culturally insensitive, theoretically flawed, and methodologically inadequate. [27]

This contention was based on the poor results of the majority of extension programmes in the Third World countries. Barring a few successes in the extension programmes in the fields of agriculture, health, nutrition and education, the overall picture was quite dismal. It was a complete failure of the much trumpeted 'trickle-down' theory as the diffusion of innovation benefited only the rich and resourceful landlords and farmers at the cost of the poor peasantry. According to Dudley Seers, [28] the reasons as to why the trickle-down theory, crucial to the success of the dominant paradigm, started losing credibility in the 70s were as follows:

1. The social problems of developed nations were spreading concerns about the environmental costs of economic growth;
2. Despite substantial transfers of capital and technology from the developed nations to the Third World, the gap between per capita incomes between the two blocs was growing;
3. Third World nations with impressive rates of growth did not achieve either the political status or social equity expected of them;
4. Income inequality was rising all over the Third World countries;
5. Unemployment rates were refusing to go down in spite of impressive growth rates;

6. Power was being concentrated among an elite coterie who benefited from the growth, who then used that power to preserve the inequality in their societies.

The dominant paradigm was also criticized for its over-emphasis on mass media's role to persuade people to achieve, maintain, and strengthen development goals. Media's role in development became paramount when UNESCO in 1960 came up with a guideline about a country's desirable per capita consumption of television sets, radio receivers, newspapers, and cinema seats.

Contrary to these expectations, the state-controlled capital-intensive mass media networks in developing countries were expanded and manipulated for political propaganda instead of meeting development objectives. Often, poverty reduction efforts were used as a promotional tool for the ruling political parties, as "champion", without enough emphasis on the real focus of creating an open and inclusive dialogue on poverty issues and translating them into policy actions. For instance, in India, the slogan of "Garibi Hatao" (Remove Poverty) given by the then Prime Minister, Mrs. Indira Gandhi, in 1971 was one such pro-Congress propaganda gimmick which was broadcast day and night by official mass media channels. In reality, almost all centrally planned development projects were rendered ineffective due to collusion between corrupt officials and political pressure groups while archaic rural social structures thwarted all attempts to reach the poorest of the poor.

Things worsened during Emergency when the entire news media including the national news agencies were gagged while radio broadcasting service and important national dailies like the Times of India were roped in for propaganda blizzard. As a result, both of them jocularly earned the derisive epithet of All 'Indira' Radio and the Times of 'Indira' respectively. Thus, the story of India was indeed the story of almost entire developing world reeling under the mounting pressure of underdevelopment.

Despite a few notable exceptions like Brazil and Korea that showed impressive increase in their GNP rates, there was no let up in the growth rates of poverty, unemployment and consequent inequality. Until the 1960s, the GNP rates in Brazil showed an annual increase of seven percent from the mid-60s, whereas in Korea, since 1974, GNP was growing at 10 percent per year. But this meant almost nothing for the poor and the downtrodden caught in the poverty trap. This downward trend meant failure of the dominant paradigm which failed to yield desired results for the following reasons: [29]

1. Quantification of Development: According to Rogers, this approach did not consider the question of equality of the benefits of development. The emphasis was on absolute growth and not its equitable distribution. The 'growth-first-and-let-equality-come-later' mentality often was justified by the trickle-down theory that leading sectors, once advances, would then spread their advantage to the lagging sectors. [30]
2. Capital-Intensive Technology: The dominant paradigm of development was to be driven by capital-intensive and labour-extensive technology. It had no room for labour-intensive industries. As a result, all the money/capital was spent in procuring foreign made machines—tool and technology—while the surplus mass of cheap labour abundantly available in these countries was conveniently abandoned. This machine and technology-intensive approach aggravated the already high unemployment rates, leading to further joblessness and deterioration in the quality of life. As the huge capital required for procuring heavy machinery was furnished by international lending agencies controlled by the developed world, the developing countries' debt burden increased to such an extent that the situation was described as economic colonialism. [31]
3. Internal Causes: Rogers's 'sub-culture of peasantry' identified several internal or in-the-head constraints to

development. He blamed the traditional nature of the Third World peasants as the main reason for the failure of the dominant paradigm.

4. Centralized Planning: Central to dominant paradigm was the role of centralized planning in development. As a result, all the Third World countries in Asia, Africa and Latin America set up national development and planning commissions. Run by economists and bankers sitting in their ivory towers, these monoliths were entrusted with the task of developing central development strategies for the whole nation. Commenting on this situation, Robert McNamara, the President of the World Bank, said in 1973: "No programme will help small farmers if it is designed by those who have no knowledge of their problems and operated by those who have no interest in their future". This top-down model of economic development failed as it did not allow a two-way, participatory and bottom-up flow of communication. Its isolationist approach had no room for self-reliance and popular participation in development activities.

The development paradigm also failed because it overlooked the social fragmentation in developing countries where the economic and political power and resources were concentrated in the hands of a small 'social elite' and large section of population had no share in political and economic decision-making whatsoever. Thus, whatever little development occurred with the help of development paradigm brought further stagnation, greater concentration of income and power in a few hands, higher unemployment rates, and an ever-widening gap between the rich and the disadvantaged sectors.

The existence of a 'dual society' in these countries reflected the quintessential conflict between the traditional and modern. The social elite constituted the modern and upwardly-mobile sector of overly ambitious Westernized English-speaking 'brown sahibs' with all the socio-economic and political power and resources concentrated in their hands. The traditional society, on the other hand, comprised the rural peasants and the rest of the population which was both poor and backward. The proponents of modernization sought to transform these traditional folks with the help of diffusion of innovation and mass media exposure. But the effort failed due to various reasons including the modern sector's tendency to dominate the traditional sector for its own vested interests.

As pointed out by Fjes, "Often times it is not in the modern sector's interest...to modernize the so called traditional sector. Rather that being isolated from the modern sector, the so-called traditional sector often exists in a relationship of oppressive dependency, its human and material resources being exploited for the benefit of the modern sector. Rather than the traditional and modern sectors existing as two distinct systems, each more or less separate within one system of economic, political and social relationships, with the modern sector dominating the traditional". [32] Thus, what the British did to India in terms of colonial and racial exploitation, the same was repeated by the native Indian social elite towards their simpleton rural folks.

Over the years, this well-entrenched social structure got further consolidated in most of the developing countries where in the name of democracy, corrupt political elite and ruling parties developed an insatiable desire to perpetuate poverty and backwardness for their petty vote bank politics. The task was made easier by the absence of education as it was easy to manipulate and exploit the illiterate and uneducated masses for their votes with gifts of cash and kind. In this respect, grant of universal suffrage without ensuring minimum educational levels of the electorate proved detrimental to the best interest of democracy in a country. For instance, in India, though the voter has become more mature and shrewd in casting his/her vote, yet this practice of vote bank politics still continues. In fact, given the growing role of money and muscle power in politics, no honest person, howsoever patriotic and earnest, can even think of winning an election these days on the merit of personal integrity alone. This perhaps is the biggest challenge before the Indian democracy today.

3.5 Opposing Paradigm: Dependency

The decade of 1960s was the period of rising frustrations as modernization failed to deliver on its promises. The condition of the poor worsened and this decline gave new fuel to the criticisms of the dominant conception of mainstream development practices, which came under fire for being culturally insensitive, theoretically flawed, and methodologically inadequate. [33] The criticism of this paradigm became so intense that even some of its most vocal proponents like Rogers had to announce the 'passing of the dominant paradigm' by mid-1970s.

Thus, abysmal failure of the mainstream dominant paradigm paved way for its opposing theory—the dependency paradigm. It emerged in Latin America in the late 1960s to early 1980s as a critique of the dominant paradigm and its modernization thesis. It was grounded in the neo-Marxist political economy approach aimed at providing an alternative framework for development not based on GNP alone. Its proponents argued that Western transnational corporations or TNCs exercised control, with the support of their respective governments, over the developing countries by setting the terms of global trade—dominating markets, resources, production, and labour.

According to dependency theorists or 'dependentistas', development for these developing countries was actually meant to strengthen the dominance of developed nations that composed the 'core' and to maintain the 'peripheral' or poor nations in a position of dependence—in other words, to make conditions suitable for 'dependent development'. In its extreme form, the outcome of such relationship was 'the development of underdevelopment'. [34]

They argued that with its exclusive economic focus, modernization failed to consider a number of historical and broader socio-political factors that impeded the autonomous development of many developing countries. Its proponents ignored elements such as colonization, past exploitation of resources, and, more recently, globalization—all of which greatly affect and limit the individual capacities of countries in the political and economic spheres.

To address this problem, they proposed a plan that worked on two levels: Nationally, developing countries on the periphery were to become economically self-reliant and less dependent on foreign imports. Internationally, they would form alliances among themselves to create a stronger political presence. The ultimate goal behind this was to change the overall international set of relationships by forming a bloc of many countries with similar aspirations. The Non-Aligned Movement's demand for a new international economic order or NIEO was a result of this solidarity.

This had a significant impact on the economic and development policies of many Third World countries, especially in the 1970s and early 1980s. This resulted in the adoption of import-substitution policies by many of those countries. The strategy aimed at protecting national industries from outside competition by subsidizing them and putting high tariffs on imported products. The main idea was to stimulate growth of domestic industries and to reduce dependence on richer countries.

3.5.1 World System Theory: Meanwhile, the oversimplified division of the world into core and periphery levels by the dependency theorists not only failed to explain fully the causes of underdevelopment but also to put forward alternative models of development. According to Worsley, by ascribing causes of underdevelopment exclusively to the centres of international capitalism, dependency theorists failed to consider relevant internal causes contributing to the problem, such as the role played by national elites. "These elites often form strategic alliances with those of the developed world, and they play a significant role in shaping, often in negative ways, the development process of their countries", says Servaes.

The dependency theorists were also criticized for their failure to pay attention to the differences in political-economic status among developing countries. This resulted in big and potentially rich emerging economies such as Brazil and India being put in the same category as much smaller and poorer ones. Wallerstein's world-system theory, though very much within the ambit of dependency theory, addresses this key concern and provides a more appropriate representation of international relations.

The world system theory of Wallerstein addresses and refines the major flaws of the dependency theory by adopting a more holistic approach, encompassing national and international dynamics within a unified world system. His historical analysis puts the origin of the modern world system in the 16th century. This world system, based on capitalism, is divided into core, dominated by a few rich countries; a periphery inhabited by many poorer countries of Africa, Asia and Latin America; and a semi-periphery, including major countries such as Brazil, India, Egypt, Mexico and others, with higher levels of resources than the majority of the developing countries. This intermediate layer, the semi-periphery, addresses the criticisms received by dependency theorists for the oversimplified division of the world into rich and poor countries. The three levels—core, periphery and semi-periphery—are contained in a unified world system operated by the mechanics of capitalism operating at national and international levels.

The main contribution of the world system theory consists of elevating the unit of analysis from the national to the international level, thus allowing a better comprehension of the global scenario. As regards communication, this theory is at par with the dependency theory with its focus on the key but narrow role of media and information flows in the overall international communication scenario. [35]

3.5.2 Many Voices, One World: Among the key issues that dominated the international scenario from the late 1960s to early

1980s was the demand for New International Economic Order or NIEO raised by the Non-Aligned Movement (NAM) that defined development as a political struggle. Linked to this demand was the issue of a New World Information and communication order or NWICO. The debates on the issue at UNESCO led to the appointment of a Commission for the Study of Communication Problems chaired by Sean MacBride. In its Report entitled, "Many Voices, One World", the MacBride Commission sought freedom of information and how media and communication technologies should be used to promote a fair and balanced flow of information against the uneven flow of media programmes and information coming from the North. This imbalance, it said, was a form of cultural imperialism that needed to be addressed.

The battle over NWICO reached its climax in 1980 when both the United States and Great Britain withdrew from UNESCO. This and other events like the fall of the Iron Curtain not only considerably weakened the bargaining power of the NAM but also made many of the issues raised by NWICO lost much of their relevance.

However, the dependency theorists remained rooted in the classic media-centric approach to communication. Despite significant differences between modernization and dependency theorists, their communication model remained same: a one-way communication flow, with main difference between the two theorists being who was controlling and sending the message and for what purpose.

3.6 The Emerging Paradigm: Participatory

Failure of the modernization and dependency paradigms led to the emergence of alternative voices and perspectives that viewed development as 'a multi-dimensional process' involving major changes in social structures, popular attitudes and national institutions, as well as the acceleration of economic growth, the reduction of inequality and the eradication of absolute poverty which meant a life degraded by denial of basic human necessities. [36] This concept laid stress on 'real development' described by political economist Denis Goulet as: "Freeing men from nature's servitude, from economic backwardness and oppressive technological institutions, from unjust class structures and political exploiters, from cultural and psychic alienation—in short, from all of life's inhuman agencies". [37]

This holistic description of real development was aimed at reducing inequalities and improving conditions of the poorest of the poor by giving people a bigger role in development efforts through participation and self-reliance. It included a clean environment, growth with equity, provision of basic needs such as food, shelter, education, and medical care, meaningful employment and relationships with others, and a harmonious relationship between culture and change.

This approach stressed people's role in shaping their own destiny and emphasized the protection of environment and culture. "Development is a process of social change which has in its goal the improvement in the quality of life of all or the majority of people without doing violence to the natural and cultural environment in which they exist, and which seeks to involve the majority of the people as closely as possible in this enterprise, making them the masters of their own destiny". [38]

Central to the participatory model of development is the basic assumption that there are no countries or communities that function completely autonomously and that are completely self-sufficient, nor are there any nations whose development is exclusively determined by external factors. Thus, it sought to provide a framework within which both the centre and the periphery could be studied separately and in their mutual relationship, both at the global, national and local levels.

At the same time, the participatory approach favoured a multiplicity of approaches based on the context and the basic, felt needs, and the empowerment of the most oppressed and disadvantaged sections of societies. It revolves around the thesis that change must be structural and occur at multiple levels in order to achieve these ends. It often transcends its scope to enhance project's results and sustainability to become a capacity-building element of a broader social dimension. According to UNDP, "Since participation requires increased influence and control, it also demands increased empowerment —in economic, social and political terms". [39]

3.6.1 Empowerment: It is defined as the expansion of assets and capabilities of poor people to participate in, negotiate with, influence, control, and hold accountable institutions that affected their lives. According to Friere, people's empowerment can be achieved through a process of awareness or 'conscientization' that requires the poor to become aware of their conditions through a totality of reflection and action. The key to achieve this kind of empowerment is communication through dialogue.

Since there can be no participation without communication, this approach promotes a more dialogic and two-way flow of communication with more interactive connotation to facilitate participation and empowerment. Hence, the top-down model of communication of the modernization paradigm gets diluted in favour of a 'bottom-up' approach with self-development of the local community as its primary focus. It includes the integrated rural development approach and re-emergence of culture in developmental activities. It also assigns new roles to a variety of communication media, including the folk media, in development. Thus, media are no longer the central element in participatory communication but one of the tools for empowerment through capacity building. It, thus, shifts the focus from media to people, from persuasion to participation.

This requires that local people or stakeholders should be engaged in the development process from the beginning to play an active role throughout the process. This implies that local people should have the power to take part in the decision-making process, since power can be conceived as the ability to shape social context.

3.6.2 Capacity Building: According to Amartya Sen, poverty is not simply an income issue but also a social issue.

Poverty leads to capability deprivation. Therefore, income poverty and capability poverty are two closely related dimensions because income greatly affects the capabilities of an individual, and vice-versa.

Poverty and capability deprivation cause social exclusion. Therefore, elimination or significant reduction in social exclusion is a step towards poverty reduction. By engaging stakeholders in the decision-making process, development communication not only reduces poor people's 'capability deprivation' but also facilitates the process of empowerment. According to World Bank, "Using dialogue to engage stakeholders in probing and assessing the situation can help break the broader vicious circle of poverty, where income cannot be earned without a proper level of individual capabilities, and individual capabilities cannot be improved while the individual remains in conditions of poverty".

3.6.3 Grassroots Organizations: Therefore, it recognizes cultural-identity and multidimensionality and stresses capacity building with the involvement of the grassroots level local organizations. It encourages freedom from external dependency by stressing self-reliance of local communities by including ecological dimension and areas like population, food, employment, human sentiments as well as science and technology.

These local organizations are important to speed up rural development through small-scale self-help development projects (SHDP). According to Uphoff and Esman, [40] 'those cases in which there was more of an organization reaching down to the local level, accountable to the local people, and involved with rural development functions have accomplished rural development objectives more successfully with respect to the available resources base than have those with less rural organization".

For instance, the local grassroots organizations in Kenya were able to achieve higher agricultural productivity and better rural welfare in areas of health, nutrition, education, security, employment, political participation, and equity in income distribution. A case study of SHDP in rural Kenya could achieve the following objectives:

1. They produced a net transfer of resources from the centre to the rural areas;
2. They appeared to foster a more equitable distribution of wealth within local communities;
3. They marshalled local initiative and entrepreneurial skills in ways the State could not do by itself;
4. Most importantly, they provided an organizational infrastructure at the grassroots level without which the development of the rural poor was unlikely to proceed.

It considers individuals as 'active agents of development efforts' instead of 'passive recipients'. Central to this approach is the contention that "if peasants do not control or share control of the processes of their own development, there can be no guarantee that it is their best interest that is being served". [41] Hence, common features of this perspective are the emphasis on people through self-reliance, the endogenous vision of development, and the attention to power and rights issues. This new concept set itself new goals to emphasize plurality and active participation of people for a meaningful and real development in the Third World. These goals [42] were:

1. Equity in distribution of information and other benefits of development. The emphasis was placed on the poorest of the poor, those living in urban slums and backward rural areas. The widening hiatus between the advantaged groups and the disadvantaged had to be closed. Growth with equity was the main focus in the 1970s.
2. Active participation of people at the grassroots: The objective was to involve the input of people in activities that were ostensibly set up for their benefit. This not only liberated the people from a spiral of silence but also ensured that development plans and decisions were relevant and meaningful to the recipients.
3. Participation for liberation through education: At the same

time, this approach was also critical of the Western education systems which were totally irrelevant to and oblivious of the real problems of the Third World. The alien education systems made the people passive and uncritical of the existing inequity in their societies. According to Paulo Freire, who advocated the idea of 'Participation for Liberation', education and communication have to be participative and receiver-centred. Rather than being top-down, the educational process has to be dialectic, helping people to understand the world around them and liberating them from the oppressive tyranny of a world view created by the elites to serve their own ends.

4. Independence of local communities (or nations) to tailor development projects to their own objectives: It stressed reliance on local human skills and material resources, thus fostering greater self-reliance in development leading to freedom from external dependency.
5. Integration of the old and new ideas, the traditional and modern systems, the endogenous and exogenous elements to constitute a unique blend suited to the needs of a particular community: This approach aimed at fostering synthesis of the modern and the traditional. Unlike dominant paradigm, it did not talk of exterminating the traditional with the imposition of modern world view. Rather, it encouraged inclusion of the native wisdom in achieving real development. [43]

3.6.4 Small is Beautiful: The participatory approach encourages efforts to develop small, alternative, people-friendly model of development as against heavy, capital-intensive technology-driven model that required massive industrialization, urbanization and centralized economic planning. This alternative was provided by British economist Schumacher in his thesis 'Small is Beautiful' [44] in which he advocated an 'intermediate technology' that employed local knowledge, resources and technique. As an effective and affordable counter to the capital-intensive modernization through industrialization that neglected small-scale rural enterprises, Schumacher's thesis favoured technology which improves labour productivity, uses local resources, minimizes the use of non-renewable resources, and produces goods for local markets. According to Weaver and Jameson, [45] it is essentially a small-scale, self-development recipe for the rural poor who have been totally marginalized in development planning. Conducive to self-reliant development at the village level, Schumacher's appropriate technology idea had several advantages as it attempted to achieve the following: [46]

1. Create employment in rural areas where most of the people live;
2. Use local skills, material and financial resources thus leading to lesser dependence on external sources;
3. Maximize use of renewable resources;
4. Be compatible with local cultures and practices; and
5. Satisfy local needs and wishes.

Thus, the participatory approach redirected development efforts towards engaging stakeholders and paid attention to previously neglected aspects of social life such as culture and education.

3.7 Basic Needs Approach

This approach focuses on the basic needs and necessities that are absolutely essential to maintain a decent life. It emphasizes both the fundamental needs of people such as *roti, kapda aur makaan* i.e. food, clothing and shelter as well as respect for human rights. Its early proponents like Mahbub Ul Haq and Holis Chenery of the World Bank, Paul Streeten, a development economist, and James Grant of the Overseas Development Council felt that usual indicators of development such as the gross national product or GNP and per capita income measures failed to give adequate information on the quality of life of individuals at the bottom of the socio-economic ladder in the Third World. According to Streeten, the basic needs approach aims at eliminating the worst aspects of poverty with the following objectives:

1. Provide adequate food and clean drinking water.
2. Provide decent shelter.
3. Provide education.
4. Provide security of livelihood.
5. Provide adequate transport.
6. Help people participate in decision-making.
7. Uphold a person's dignity and self-respect.

Since, basic needs may be met in ways that deny basic rights, and human rights may be practiced in ways that may reject basic needs, Streeten added one more human right: the socio-economic right to international resources. This included the right to universal primary education; the right to adequate food and health standards; the right to equitable employment; and the right to minimum wages and collective bargaining. [47]

3.8 Integrated Rural Development

Another key feature of the participatory approach to development is the Integrated Rural Development Programme (IRDP) to simultaneously eliminate all existing constraints to development. The idea for IRDP was given by Robert McNamara, the World Bank President, who in his seminal study distinguished between relative poverty and absolute poverty. While relative poverty underlined the inequality in the distribution and consumption of resources between and within nations, absolute poverty meant a life degraded by denial of basic human necessities. He, therefore, proposed reorientation of development policies from mere economic growth to equitable distribution of the fruits of economic growth. This meant a shift away from GNP to meeting basic needs of the poorest of the poor.

In a speech calling for New Directions in Development to overcome stalemate in development approaches, [48] McNamara proposed integrated rural development to simultaneously tackle all the existing constraints to socio-economic development.

This broad-fronted approach to development planning soon became a full-fledged movement in the 1970s. Various multilateral and bilateral agencies such as the FAO, IBRD and USAID along with several national governments including that of India put together multi-package programmes to overcome constraints to development. These included measures such as:

1. Acceleration of land and tenancy reforms;
2. Better access to credit;
3. Assured availability of clean water;
4. Expansion of extension services and applied research;
5. Greater access to public services;
6. Organizational changes and new forms of rural institutions;
7. Popular participation in development decision-making;
8. Involvement of local leadership in programme planning;
9. Decentralization of authority to rural community. [49]

3.9 The Role of Culture

Unlike the modernization approach to development that pooh-poohed tradition and traditional culture, the participatory approach believed in its innate potential to mobilize and motivate the rural masses. It views culture as an 'open system' in constant interaction with other elements in a society undergoing change. [50] It stresses the importance of cultural identity of local communities and of democratization of participation at all levels—international, national, local and individual. Paulo Freire refers to this as the right of the people to individually and collectively speak their word: "This is not the privilege of some few men, but the right of every woman. Consequently, no one can say it for another, in a prescriptive act, which robs others of their words".

Hence, this approach strongly refutes the stereotypical view that culture was in constant conflict with modernity held by the proponents of modernization. It was countered with the example of Japan's unique economic success achieved through fine blending of industrialism and feudal social structure.

However, the most outstanding examples of how culture could be used to bring about social change and development were provided by Mahatma Gandhi in India and the Sarvodaya Shramadana Movement in Sri Lanka. According to Melkote, Mahatma Gandhi used traditional cultural symbolic systems to propagate new ideas, behaviours, and values among the masses.

He used his stature as a holy man to bring about several social reforms. Similarly, the Sri Lankan Sarvodaya Movement, a self-help organization, worked on the philosophy of self-reliance, self-development, grassroots development, popular participation, maintenance of ecological balance, and the importance of culture in social development. [51] As a facilitator of development, it made active use of local culture, traditional forms and philosophies of communication to meet user needs in the rural and other areas where the problems exist.

Hence, the priorities of the participatory approach, well beyond the economic dimension, are reflected in aforementioned areas of concern as well as the Millennium Development Goals and the Sustainable Development Goals enshrined in the 2030 Agenda. Most development priorities, with people's participation and capacity-building as the main focus, are outlined within political framework based on adherence to good governance and democratic principles that includes freedom and human rights.

As a result, most development programmes carry the participatory mark. However, wide convergence in multiple participatory approaches, have not resulted in a unified paradigm. Rather, it has generated a number of theoretical perspectives such as: the multiplicity paradigm (Servaes, 1991); the empowerment approach (Friedmann, 1992); another development (Melkote, 1991); the autonomous development (Carmen, 1996); and other conceptions of participatory, people-based development. Thus, the participatory model works within the framework of multiplicity.

3.10 Types of Participation

In 1995, the World Bank identified four types of participation such as: (a) information sharing, (b) consultation, (c) Collaboration, and (d) empowerment. Of these, the first two i.e. information sharing and consultation are considered low-level forms of participation, while the other two i.e. collaboration and empowerment are considered high-level forms. According to Mefalopulos, [52] these types are consistent with others including: (i) passive participation, when stakeholders attend meetings to be informed; (ii) participation by consultation, when stakeholders are consulted but the decision-making rests in the hands of the experts; (iii) functional participation, where stakeholders are allowed to have some input, although not necessarily from the beginning of the process and not in equal partnership; and (iv) empowered participation, when relevant stakeholders take part throughout the whole cycle of the development initiative and have an equal influence in the decision-making process.

However, the best known and most relevant participatory approach is rural participatory appraisal or RPA. It gained prominence in the 1980s as a research method that aimed to reach a balance between researchers' needs to be scientific in their approach and community's rights to participate in activities concerning their own well-being. RPA promotes a number of participatory techniques and tools that require no literacy skills to encourage the most disadvantaged, often illiterate, rural poor to express their knowledge and ideas openly.

Thanks to its working method, the RPA has enormous empowering potential. It works two ways: (a) it facilitates people's involvement in the problem-analysis process; and (b) stimulates the 'reversal of learning' from the rural poor to the experts. This way, it helps in the empowerment of the poorest and the most disadvantaged sectors of the society, which often tend to be in rural areas or on the periphery of rural-urban divide. While RPA focuses on self reliance of the most disadvantaged sections of the society, the other well-known approaches such as participatory action research or PAR and community-driven development or CDD aim at putting communities and local stakeholders in the driving seats of development efforts.

3.11 Participatory Research

The participatory approach and its research methodology allows growing role for local stakeholders and indigenous knowledge in the problem-analysis and problem-solving processes of development initiatives. Based on capacity building and empowerment of people and communities, its strength comes from plurality and multiplicity. According to Servaes, [53] participatory research calls for "an upward, transactive, open and radical form of planning that encompasses both grassroots collective action and large-scale processes. This kind of planning and research is centrally conceived with human growth, learning processes through mobilization and the basic aim is to involve the people under study cooperatively in the planning and research process, with the planner or researcher as a facilitator and participant". The characteristics of participatory research have been defined as follows:

1. It rests on the assumption that human beings have an innate ability to create knowledge and that this is not the prerogative of 'professionals'.
2. It is an educational process for the participants in the research programme as well as for the researcher. It involves the identification of community needs, awareness regarding constraints, an analysis of the causes of glitches and the designing and execution of solutions.
3. There is a conscious commitment of the researcher to work for the cause of the community. Thus, the traditional scientific principle of neutrality is rejected in this research.
4. It is based on a dialectical process of dialogue between the researcher and the community. Dialogue provides a

framework which guards against manipulation from outside and serves as a means of control by the community over the direction of the research process.

5. It is a problem-solving approach. The aim is to discover the causes of problems and mobilize the creative human potential to solve social problems by changing the underlying conditions to those problems.
6. Its major asset is its heuristic value. The close communication between the researcher and the community fosters an atmosphere in which all participants analyse the social environment and formulate plans of action. [54]

Thus, the strength of its research methodology lies in its innate flexibility in adapting to a situation. The resultant benefits accrued from the adoption of participatory approach to development are: (a) services can be provided at a lower cost; (b) participation has intrinsic values for participants, alleviating feelings of alienation and powerlessness; (c) participation is a catalyst for further development efforts; (d) participation leads to a sense of responsibility for the project; and (e) participation ensures the use of indigenous knowledge and expertise.

Endnotes

1. Melkote, S.R. (1991), "Communication for Development in the Third World: Theory and Practice", New Delhi: Sage Publications.
2. Ibid.
3. Portes, Alejandro (1976), "On the Sociology of National Development: Theories and Issues", *American Journal of Sociology*, 82(1).
4. Ibid.
5. Deutsch, Karl (1961), "Social Mobilization and Political Development", *American Political Science Review*, 55.
6. Portes, 1976.
7. Inkeles, Alex (1969), "Making Men Modern: On the Causes and Consequences of Individual Change in Six Countries", *American Journal of Sociology*, 75, September.
8. Melkote, 1991.
9. Rogers, 1976c: 49.

10. Madhok, Balraj, "Nationalism, Democracy and Social Change", New Delhi, Deepak Prakashan.
11. Golding, Peter (1974), "Media Role in National Development: Critique of a Theoretical Orthodoxy", *Journal of Communication*, 24(3), pp. 39-53.
12. Rogers, Everett M. and Ronny Adhikarya (1979), "Diffusion of Innovations: An Up-to-Date Review and Commentary" in Dam Nmmo (ed.), 'Communication Year Book 3', pp. 67-81, New Jersey: International Communication Association.
13. Rogers, Everett M. (1969), "Modernisation among Peasants", New York: Holt, Rinehart and Winston.
14. Ibid.
15. Ibid.
16. Rogers, Everett M. and F.F. Shoemaker (1971), "Communication of Innovations: A Cross Cultural Approach", New York: The Free Press.
17. Katz, Elihu (1963), "The Diffusion of New Ideas and Practices", in Wilbur Schramm (ed.), 'The Science of Human Communication', New York: Basic Books.
18. Ibid.
19. Katz, Elihu and Paul F. Lazarsfeld (1955), "Personal Influence: The Part Played by People in the Flow of Mass Communications", New York: Free Press.
20. Tard, Gabriel (1903), "The Laws of Imitation", New York: Holt.
21. Melkote, S.R. (1991), "Communication for Development in the Third World: Theory and Practice", New Delhi: Sage Publications.
22. Ibid.
23. Ibid.
24. Weaver, James H. and Kenneth Jameson (1978), "Economic Development: Competing Paradigms, Competing Parables", Washington D.C.: Development Studies Programme, Agency for International Development.
25. Melkote, Srinivas R. (1991), "Communication for Development in the Third World", New Delhi: Sage Publications.
26. Adelman, I. and C.T. Morris (1973), "Economic Growth and Social Equity in Developing Countries", California: Stanford University Press.
27. Servaes, J. (1991).
28. Seers, Dudley (1977), "The Meaning of Development",

International Development Review, XIX (2), pp. 2-7.

29. Melkote, 1991.
30. Rogers, 1976.
31. Oshima, Harry, T. (1976), "Development and Mass Communication: A Re-Examination" in W. Schramm and D. Lerner (eds.), 'Communication and Change', pp. 17-30, Honolulu: University Press of Hawai.
32. Fjes, Fred (1976), "Communication and Development", unpublished paper, College of Communications, University of Illinois: Urbana-Champaign.
33. Servaes, Jan (1991).
34. Gunder, Frank, A. (1969), "Capitalism and Underdevelopment in Latin America", New York: Monthly Review Press
35. Thussu, D.K. (2000), "International Communication: Continuity and Change", London: Arnold.
36. McNamara, Robert (1973), "Bell Weather Speech on New Directions in Development", World Bank.
37. Goulet, Denis (1971), "The Cruel Choice: A New Concept in Theory of Development", New York: Atheneum.
38. Wang, Georgette and Wimal Dissanayake (1984), "Culture, Development and Change: Some Explorative Observations", in G. Wang and W. Dissanaye (eds.), 'Continuity and Change in Communication Systems' New Jersey: Ablex.
39. UNDP Annual Report, 1993.
40. Uphoff, Norman and M. Esman (1974), "Local Organisations for Rural Development: Analysis of Asian Experience", New York: Centre for International Studies, Cornell University.
41. Ascroft, Joseph and Sipho Masilela (1989), "From Top-Down to Co-Equal Communication: Popular Participation in Development Decision-Making", paper presented at the seminar on Participation: A Key Concept in Communication and Change, Pune: University of Poona.
42. Rogers, Everett M. (1976), "The Passing of the Dominant Paradigm: Reflections on Diffusion Research", in W. Schramm and D. Lerner (eds.), 'Communication and Change', Honolulu: University Press Hawaii.
43. Hedebrao, Goran (1982), "Communication and Social Change in Developing Nations: A Critical View", Ames: Iowa State University Press.
44. Schumacher, E.F. (1973), "Small is Beautiful", New York:

Harper and Row.

45. Weaver, James H. and Kenneth Jameson (1978), "Economic Development: Competing Paradigms, Competing Parables", Washington D.C.: Development Studies Programme, Agency for International Development.
46. Dunn, P.D. (1978), "Appropriate Technology", New York: Schocken Books.
47. Streeten, Paul (1979), "Development Ideas in Historical Perspective" in Kim Q. Hill (ed.), 'Toward a New Strategy for Development', New York: Pergamon Press.
48. World Bank, 1973.
49. Ibid.
50. Wang, Georgette and Wimal Dissanayake (1984), "Culture, Development and Change: Some Explorative Observations", in G. Wang and W. Dissanaye (eds.), 'Continuity and Change in Communication Systems', New Jersey: Ablex.
51. Dissanayake, W. (1984), "A Buddhist Approach to Development: A Sri Lankan Endeavour", in G. Wang and W. Dissanayake (eds.), 'Continuity and Change in Communication Systems', New Jersey: Ablex.
52. Mefalupulos, 2003.
53. Servaes, Jan (1989), "Participatory Communication Research within Social Movement", paper presented at the seminar on Participation: A Key Concept in Communication for Change and Development, Pune: University of Poona.
54. Kronenburg, J. (1986), "Empowerment of the Poor: A Comparative Analysis of Two Development Endeavours in Kenya", cited in Jan Servaes, 1989.

4

Communication Approach to Development

Theories in communication for development fall under two broad categories. First are those that come within the ambit of dominant paradigm of modernization such as communication and the modernization theory and the diffusion of innovations theory. The second category of alternative post-modernist paradigm has the participatory communication and action research model of self-reliance and empowerment.

4.1 Communication: The Essential Human Connection

Communication as a relating tool provides the essential human connection for the mankind to survive. Man being a social animal, the need for communication is as necessary to existence as life and as basic as hunger for food and water for survival. It is both a natural individual demand and a requirement for social existence to use communication resources in order to engage in the sharing of experience through words and symbols.

According to Indian tradition, in the beginning of creation was 'Aum' or the 'Word', the first sound ever made or heard. It is also called the *'shabda brahman'* or the 'Word Divine'. It is also called the Naad Brahma in Yoga. The world communication is derived from Latin *communis* which means 'common'. Thus, communication is a process which increases commonality but also requires elements of commonality for it to occur at all. [1] Hencc, synonyms like interaction, interchange, dialogue, sharing, communion and commonness are often used to define communication.

However, according to Indian communication theory, communication by itself does not increase commonality nor does it need commonality for occurrence. For instance, a common language does not necessarily bring people together.

There are other factors like culture that bring about a sense of commonality and a sense of community.

The Indian theory of communication originates from the word *Sadharanikaran* [2] which is derived from the Sanskrit word *Sadharan* meaning simple, common or ordinary. Sadharanikaran thus implies simplification. The word has a familiar ring and is equivalent to the Latin word 'communis' that is communication, meaning commonness of experience. Sadharanikaran has been vividly described in Bharata's Natya Shastra, also known as the fifth Veda. It was discovered in the 10th century A.D. by Bhattanayak.

Now how does Sadharanikaran take place?

According to Bharat, Sadharanikaran is that point in the climax of a drama when the audience becomes one with the actor who lives an experience through his acting on stage and starts simultaneously reliving the same experience. The process has been described as *rasa swadan* i.e. tasting the same flavour or relish. When Sadharanikaran happens, universalisation or commonness of experience takes place. Universalisation leads to identification and involvement. Whatever is communicated leaves a deep impact. Now, this process of universalisation can take place only among *Sahridayas*. Derived from the Sanskrit word *Hridaya* meaning heart, a sahridaya is a person in a state of emotional ecstasy similar to that of the sender or communicator of the message. In this respect, both the sender and the recipient of the message become co-equals or sahridayas literally meaning 'of one heart'.

Thus, communication here is a relationship based on common and mutual understanding and feeling. Communication thus presupposes a shared symbolic environment, a social relationship or social interaction, among those who participate in it.

Therefore, human communication is a society-wide process that can take place at different levels. [3] McQuail has shown these levels in the form of a pyramid of communication. At the base of this pyramid is the intrapersonal level of communication that stands for processing of information (for instance, attention, perception, comprehension, recall and learning) and its possible effects (on knowledge, opinion and attitude). The next is the interpersonal level where attention is usually given to forms of conversation and patterns of interaction, influence, affiliation and normative control (for e.g., dyad, couple).

This holds true of the third level of intra-group (for instance, family) where there are even more and more varied types of communication network, based on some shared features of daily life: an environment (such as neighbourhood), an interest (such as music), a need (such as the care of small children) or an activity (such as a sport).

At this level, the key questions that arise include attachment and identity, cooperation and norm formation. The next is the institutional or organization level of communication process (for e.g. political system or business firm). The activities here are very diverse and require correlation along with communication. The last level of communication process or the apex point in this pyramid is that of the whole society where the society-wide network of mass communication works.

Hence, the process of human communication is simple, linear and effects-oriented. It involves sending of meaningful messages from one person (source) to another (receiver). These messages could be oral or written, visual or olfactory. Even things such as laws, customs, practices, ways of dressing, gestures, buildings, gardens, military parades and even flags have a communication purpose and design, says McQuail. "Human communication", according to Ashley Montagu and Floyd Matson, "is a clash of symbols and it covers a multitude of signs. But it is more than media and message, information and persuasion; it also meets a deeper need and serves a higher purpose. Whether clear or garbled, tumultuous or silent, deliberate or fatally inadvertent, communication is the ground of meeting and the foundation of community. It is, in short, the essential human connection".

4.2 Concept of Development Communication

Also called "communication for development", "development support communication, and "communication for social change", development communication, "is the art and science of human communication applied to the speedy transformation of a country and the mass of its people from poverty to a dynamic state of economic growth that makes possible greater social equality and the larger fulfilment of the human potential. [4] Communication is a relating tool necessary for development and social change through infusion of new ideas, skills and techniques. Often described as a 'communication with a social conscience', development communication, with its horizontal dialogue-based interpersonal approach, aims at ensuring mutual understanding between the agency and various stakeholders by investigating issues before other forms of communication can take place.

As a concept, communication for development or development-support communication had almost parallel beginning with the conceptual framework for development soon after the Second World War. The rise of communication sciences in 1950s gave it further fillip and recognition as an academic discipline. It was popularized by the UN and its various executive agencies like the UNDP, UNICEP and FAO. It was also supported by multilateral funding agencies like the World Bank and the IMF.

Its origin can be traced back to diffusion study of hybrid corn by American agricultural scientists Ryan and Cross in 1942 when their research firmly established the critical role of technological information for increased farm production. Soon, agricultural extension education, as a part of agricultural sciences, branched off as a specialized field to help evolve theory and practice of modern methods of agriculture. It was found to be particularly useful in helping the poor and marginalized farmers of developing countries who were still dependent on subsistence methods of farming. It was, therefore, considered necessary to help them change their traditional agricultural practices for better ones and increase their output through extension methods.

This approach of spreading innovation, new ideas, practices and technologies in agriculture to the farmers in developing countries came to be known as agricultural extension in the 1950s. In view of the heavy dependence of agricultural extension on communication techniques and methodologies, communication for agricultural extension came to be known as 'agricultural communication'. This gave recognition to development communication not only as a specialized area of communication but also as an academic discipline. It became popular among development agencies and slowly diversified into rural communication when extension specialists began to work as change agents to influence adoption decisions in a desired manner.

The extension workers were given the task of convincing people through persuasive communication to change their attitude in favour of innovation or technology. Thus, began a one-way flow of influence-oriented messages from change agencies at the top to the rural peasantry at the bottom. It was also known as the top-down communication or the 'Pro-Persuasion Model of Development' where persuasive extension communication was utilized to persuade individuals and nations for adoption of technological innovations.

However, a contrarian view was given by John L. Woods in 1976 who conceived of a triangular nexus with three points namely the knowledge generators, political leaders and development-knowledge users to show the routes of communication that were not only vertical from top to bottom and bottom to upwards, but also horizontal between the institutions and persons connected with the process of development and social change.

4.3 Development Communication for Modernization

Through its exploratory and participatory approach, development communication seeks to play modernizing role in rural communities. In this context, communication for development is more than just a dialogue between the source of the message and its receiver. Instead, it fulfils certain social functions which are as follows.

4.3.1 Transforming Role: Communication for development aims at making people believe that it is possible to achieve a better and higher quality of life by adapting to new innovations and situations. For this to happen, a person needs to have a 'mobile personality' [5] i.e. he/she must be equipped with a high capacity for identification with new aspects of his/her environment and internalizes the new demands made by the larger society. In other words, this person has a high degree of empathy which is essentially the capacity to see oneself in other's situation.

Empathy, according to Lerner, fulfils two important functions. Firstly, it enables a person to operate efficiently in the modern society which is constantly changing and renewing itself with every new innovation and invention. Secondly, it works as an 'indispensable skill' for individuals keen to move out of their traditional settings characterized by a feudal system with regard to ownership of land, hierarchy based on kinship, a barter economy, etc.

Empathy allows the individual to internalize the process of modernization by not only being able to cope with change, but expecting and demanding it. It is the psychic nexus of all the attitudes and behaviour necessary in a modern society. Empathy, for instance endows a person with the capacity to imagine himself as a proprietor of a big grocery store in a city, to wear nice clothes and live in a nice house, to be interested in 'what is going on in the world' and to 'get out of his hole'. Thus, the role of imagination to visualize oneself as someone better off or to aspire for something different is almost as important as that of communication which plays the role of a harbinger of new ideas from outside.

4.3.2 Socializing Role: Modernization, according to Lerner, was essentially Westernization. It recapitulated the development experience of West Europe and North America from a feudal and traditional stage to modern-military-industrial societies. This social development model consisted of the following elements such as: (i) a core of mobile individuals whose psychological orientation made it easier to accept rapid changes in their personal lives and the overall social system, (ii) an omnipotent mass media system that reinforced and accelerated societal and individual change by disseminating the new ideas and attitudes conducive to development, and (iii) the correlations between the important indices of urbanization, literacy, media exposure, and economic and political participation to establish a modern Western-type society.

Under the socializing role of development communication, a mobile personality person would be then encouraged to step out of his traditional settings and try to adjust in modern milieu. Interestingly, this was something which Macaulay had already experimented, albeit in a different context, with highly ambitious, upwardly mobile social elites in colonial India. The importance given to aristocratic, foreign educated and English speaking 'Brown Sahibs', often decried as the 'coloured clones' of white Englishmen or 'Gora Sahibs'during the British Raj, marked the origin of modernization drive through Westernization. The highly anglicized class of brown sahibs, including Nehru, was like an island within the vast societal sea of traditional India.

Through these transforming and socializing roles, development communication helps in creating a favourable environment for the adoption of innovation and aspirations of a new identity. As has been seen, this environment is of two kinds. First, is the physical environment and second is the psychological environment. The physical environment relates to the outer periphery in which information about a new product or technique can be communicated by word of mouth or shown through posters, hoardings or graffiti on the walls. Second, is the psychological environment that concerns mind and psyche? Through persuasive communication, the target audience can be enthused to act in a desired manner by arousing empathy for something better and higher in life, says Lerner.

Based on their capacity to influence opinion among their peers, opinion leaders have been classified as polymorphic and monomorphic. Polymorphism is the degree to which an individual acts as an opinion leader for a variety of topics and issues. Its opposite, monomorphism, is the tendency for an individual to act as an opinion leader for only a single topic or issue. [6]

4.4 Communication for Diffusion of Innovation

Diffusion is the process by which an innovation is communicated through certain channels over time among the members of a social system. It is a special type of communication where the message is concerned with new idea/s. It is a communication process in which information is created and shared between sender and receiver to reach a mutual understanding. This definition implies that communication is a process of convergence (or divergence) as two or more individuals exchange information in order to move towards each other (or apart) in the meanings that they ascribe to certain events. This communication is a two-way process of convergence, rather than a one-way, linear act in which one individual seeks to transfer a message to another.

This approach describes certain communication acts or events involved in diffusion, such as when a change agent seeks to persuade a client to adopt an innovation. Considering what happened before and after this exchange, the aforementioned communication process remains only a part of the total process in which information is exchanged between the two individuals. For example, the client may come to a change agent with a problem and an innovation or an idea is recommended as a possible solution. This interaction may continue for several cycles in a process of information exchange. This process makes diffusion, according to Rogers, [7] a special type of communication, in which the messages are concerned with a new idea. It is this newness of the idea in the message content of communication that gives diffusion a special character. The newness means that some degree of uncertainty is involved.

"Uncertainty is the degree to which a number of alternatives are perceived with respect to the occurrence of an event and the relative probability of these alternatives. Uncertainty implies a lack of predictability, of structure, of information. In fact, information represents one of the main means of reducing uncertainty. Information is a difference in matter-energy that affects uncertainty in a situation where a choice exists among a set of alternatives...A technological innovation embodies information and thus reduces uncertainty about cause-effect relationships in problem solving. For instance, my adoption of residential solar panels for water heating reduces my uncertainty about future price increases in the cost of oil. We find it useful to conceptualize the diffusion and adoption of innovations in terms of a framework based on information and uncertainty. The use of these key concepts helps us to understand the diffusion of technological innovations as one type of communication process". [8]

Thus, diffusion is a process by which new ideas are inducted into a social system. Here, the term diffusion, which is the spontaneous and unplanned spread of new ideas, is different from the concept of dissemination which is directed and managed. For instance, news is disseminated while new ideas about methods, tools and techniques are diffused. Often, both the terms are used interchangeably by communication scholars to denote the planned as well as the spontaneous spread of new ideas as in social marketing.

4.4.1 Social Marketing: Based on diffusion model, social marketing entails adopting principles of marketing to promote social causes. Social marketing, according to Philip Kotler, is the design, implementation, and control of programmes seeking to increase the acceptability of a social idea or cause in a target group. It utilizes the concepts of market segregation, consumer research, concept development, communication facilitation, incentives and exchange theory to maximize target group response". [9]

The diffusion approach within modernization paradigm has also been concerned with acceptability of a social idea or cause in a target group. In this respect, the stated objectives and methods of diffusion of innovations approach overlap with those of social marketing. Both are essentially concerned with the dissemination and adoption of innovations—new ideas, new practices, products, methods, techniques and programmes. While the diffusion scholars approach their subject with a humanist and non-profit point of view, the social marketing advocates base their thesis upon a body of literature which has overriding profit-making motivations. Yet, the diffusion and social marketing approaches converge at a point where the techniques and methods evolved in the marketing field can be applied to social causes, social movements and philanthropic organizations.

Social marketing, therefore, is the explicit use of marketing skills to help translate present social action efforts into more effectively designed and communicated programmes that elicit desired audience responses. The marketing techniques are the bridging mechanism between the simple process of knowledge and the socially useful implementation of what knowledge allows, says Kotler. [10] In other words, social marketing is meticulous adaptation of the marketing methodology to social imperatives with the objectives of effecting a social change.

Four basic approaches to social change have been identified. They are—the legal, technological, economic and informational approaches. For instance, take the case of family planning. The legal approach in this case would be to pass laws to make family planning absolutely essential for all Indians as well as trespassers like the Rohingyas and

Bangladeshis. And, it must be enforced strictly. If needed, these illegal migrants should be appropriately punished for defiling the demographics of our country. The technological approach would be innovating high quality, cost-effective contraceptive and other measures to make them accessible to one and all. The economic approach would be to make sterilization for birth control free of cost and the information approach would be to inform and educate people about the ill-effects of large families for society and country.

Thus, social marketing provides a rich conceptual system for thinking through the problems of bringing about changes in the ideas or practices of a target public. The adoption of an idea, like the adoption of any product, requires a clear understanding of the target audience's needs, perceptions, preferences, reference groups, and behavioural patterns. This helps in tailoring of messages, evaluating media costs and facilities to maximize the case of adopting the idea.

4.5 The Role of Persuasion

The success of development communication largely depends on the role of persuasion which is described as the art of winning friends and influencing people. A successful persuasive communication leads to voluntary acceptance of the persuader's message by building trust. It helps in assessing risks, exploring opportunities and facilitating sharing of knowledge, experiences and perceptions. A persuasive two-way communication, therefore, plays a key role in the success and sustainability of a development initiative.

Development involves not only the transfer of technology but also communication of new ideas and skills for the successful adoption of innovations. According to Rogers, given the fact that an innovation or a new idea exists, communication about it must take place if the innovation is to spread beyond its inventor. Here, the role of persuasion through 'interpersonal communication' is particularly important for motivating people to discard their old traditional ways and opt for new technologies during the process of diffusion at the local level. This is because it involves a face-to-face exchange or communication between two or more individuals. As has been shown by a majority of diffusion studies, most individuals or potential adopters mainly depend upon a subjective evaluation of an innovation by those who have already adopted the innovation.

In this context, an analysis of the near-peer communication experience by Lazarsfeld and Merton [11] suggested that the transfer of ideas occur most frequently between two individuals who are alike or similar or homophilus. The term homophily is derived from the Greek word homoios, meaning alike or equal. Thus, homophily literally means affiliation or communication with a similar person. This concept and its opposite, heterophily is defined as the degree to which pairs of individuals who interact are different in certain attributes such as beliefs, education, social status etc. Interpersonal communication between like-minded homophilous persons who share personal and social characteristics is more likely to be meaningful and effective. On the contrary, it is generally seen that exchange of ideas or innovations is more likely to encounter problems when the communication takes place between participants who are heterophilous in nature and traits.

4.6 Role of Communication Channels

The most important element in the diffusion process, apart from an innovation, is the need for a communication channel. This channel connects or links the inventor or knowledgeable person with the intended recipient. A communication channel therefore is a means by which messages gets exchanged from the inventor to the user. In this respect, the mass media channels (both print and broadcast) are the most rapid and efficient means of informing an audience of potential adopters about the efficacy of the innovation.

Research has shown that mass media channels are relatively more effective at the knowledge stage while interpersonal channels are more reliable at the persuasion stage in the innovation-decision process. It was also found that "a temporal sequence is involved in agricultural communication in that messages are sent out through media directed to awareness, then to groups, and finally to individuals. A farmer upsetting this sequence in any way prejudices progress at some point in the adoption process". [12]

A comparative analysis of the role played by mass media and interpersonal channels in the innovation-decision process in the United States, Canada, India, Bangladesh and Colombia proved that mass media channels are of relatively greater importance at the knowledge function in both developing and developed countries. [13] For instance, mass media channels such as farm magazines, bulletins and container labels were more effective than interpersonal channels in spreading awareness about the innovation among farmers at Iowa, USA. However, in countries and regions where mass media availability was poor, their effect could not be evaluated. In Bangladesh, for instance, it was found that because mass media channels were seldom available in villages, the widespread use of cosmopolite interpersonal channels played the role similar to that performed by mass media channels in more developed countries.

An analysis of communication channels by adopter categories has further indicated that mass media channels are relatively more important than interpersonal channels for earlier adopters than for later adopters. This is because the early adopters do not require motivation by interpersonal channels as they already possess a need for innovativeness and the mass media message is enough to make them take a favourable pro-innovation decision. However, this is not the case with late adopters who go by the local experience gained through interpersonal communication with their near peers. Even, the role of opinion leaders who wield considerable influence at the community level is found to be very effective in influencing and directing behavioural change towards desired direction.

4.6.1 Communication Impact: Thus, in dominant paradigm, communication emerged as an important link through which new ideas from outside entered the local communities during the diffusion process. It was also proved beyond doubt that persuasive communication was integral to the successful implementation of dominant paradigm based on modernization approach by which 'individuals change from a traditional way of life to a more complex, technologically advanced, and rapidly changing style of life'. [14]

As the responsibility for diffusion communication was exclusively entrusted to extension services, the extension communication approach suffered severe limitations on account of shortage of staff. The extension services completely relied on interpersonal or face-to-face communication between the agent and the client. Shortage of extension workers made it all the more difficult to reach the large number of peasants spread all over the developing world. Also, the extension workers were essentially subject-matter specialists (agriculture, health etc.) and lacked communication skills required at interpersonal or intra-group levels of communication to convince the farmers. "So, extension tended to focus its attention mainly on the closest, most receptive, and thus, easiest to convince individuals who, as a class, as diffusion studies were to show later, had more education than the rest", opined Rogers. Thus, the individuals so reached were very few. Needed was a great multiplier like mass media. This need was further reinforced by the advent of radio's new avatar—the cheap and portable battery-powered transistor. As the immense power potential of radio to weld the nation together in solidarity was proved during the war years, the invention of transistor radio in the 1950s, promised great hopes for social good.

4.7 Mass Media as Magic Multiplier

Development, according to Schramm, is measured in terms of improvement in the lives of the people and strengthening of the family's or individual's capacity to deal with the rest of the society and of the nation's capacity to deal with the world. Here, mass media can play the role of a 'magic multiplier' in bringing about social change of great magnitude.

Hailing the importance of information, he emphasized that besides their modernizing effect, the mass media with their content hold the key to development. Information was seen as the much needed missing link in the development chain. In his influential book, 'Mass Media and National Development' (1964), Schramm noted how "villages in the Third World were drowsing in their traditional patterns of life...the urge to develop economically and socially usually comes from seeing how the well-developed countries or the more fortunate people live". Thus, mass media with their proven potential for information dissemination functioned as a 'bridge to a wider world'. [15]

4.7.1 Human Resource Mobilization: As the previous experience of extension workers had shown, only a minority of few educated individuals were actually receptive to new ideas and innovations while the majority of uneducated and illiterate was not. This led some scholars to opine that the real problem in developing countries was not a shortage of natural resources but underdevelopment of human resources. Therefore, human resource development through education was seen as a major challenge as modernization of industry and resources also required mobilization of human resources. According to Schramm, "the task of the mass media of information and the 'new media' of education is to speed and ease the long, slow social transformation required for economic development, and, in particular, to speed and smooth the task of mobilizing human resources behind the national effort". [16]

Earlier, Lerner had also closely examined the correlation between development and expansion of economic activity with literacy and mass media use. His findings suggested that the spread of literacy in an urban milieu and the emergence of a mobile personality highly empathetic to modernizing influences provided the means to create within the Third World societies, a climate of change. Implicit in this formulation, and in those of Wilbur Schramm who followed him, was the belief that literacy and mass media would enable the slumbering masses in the Third World to opt for change by unshackling the bonds of traditionalism leading to a process called the passing of traditional society by Lerner.

Hence, the mass media intervention was indispensable for creating a climate of modernization for social change. Both Lerner and Schramm viewed mass media as powerful 'agents and indices of modernization'. Mass media were considered the prime mover in social development. This perception was based on the impressive example of mobile transistor radio for propaganda purposes in the two World Wars. Radio, with its vast reach and mobile personality, could influence and mobilize 'passive' listeners all across the war theatre. The success of British propaganda during the First World War—on which the head of Hitler's Propaganda Ministry Josef Goebelles modelled his propaganda efforts—encouraged the belief that general public was vulnerable to propaganda and can be manipulated accordingly.

By the time, the Nazis came to power in Germany in 1933, radio broadcasting had become an extension of international diplomacy. "Real broadcasting is true propaganda. Propaganda means fighting on all battlefields of the spirit, generating, multiplying, destroying, exterminating, building and undoing", said Goebelles. [17]

The Second World War saw an explosion in international broadcasting as a propaganda tool on both sides. Prominent broadcasters of the time like the British BBC, the American Voice of America (VOA), Radio Moscow, Radio Free Europe and Radio Liberty carried on the propaganda battle during the Cold War era.

4.8 Mass Media Effects: The Power Potential

Mass media are regarded as effective instruments of power

and influence on account of their great reach and impact. This gives them an enormous capacity to sway and mobilize masses. Often, this power is seen as a two-edged knife which, if used positively, could be a source of immense benefit to the society, or else, an instrument of negative propaganda, coercion of human values and subversion of democracy.

Mass media's power potential was evident in the way it attracted and directed public attention; persuaded in matters of opinion and belief and influenced the behaviour of the target audience. This led Harold Lasswell to conceptualize mass media effects as 'direct, powerful and uniform' in his verbal model—WHO says WHAT in which CHANNEL to WHOM and with what EFFECT. [18]

Lasswell's model reinforced the belief that under the right circumstances, mass media could stimulate a specific behaviour amongst media audience termed as masses on account of their large size. These masses were seen as made up of isolated and defenceless individuals seen as passive dupes or couch potatoes who could be easily manipulated.

Based on this conceptualization, he also developed a paradigm known as the 'hypodermic needle' theory of mass communication effects. This theory is also known as the 'bullet theory'. In this theory, the mass media were the guns and the messages the bullets which were shot at passive and defenceless audiences. Similarly, in the hypodermic needle theory, the medicine was the media content injected into the veins of the passive audiences who offered no resistance whatsoever.

This idea was rooted in behavioural psychology which, in turn, was influenced by the unilinear evolutionary perspective of the social theorists. It viewed human behaviour as a more sophisticated version of animal behaviour and considered human learning to be the same as animal learning in that it responds to the stimuli of rewards and punishment. This assumption led to the stimulus-response model according to which, every stimulus or message produced a definite response in the receiver. This eventually led to the public service broadcasting by radio and television for development communication.

4.8.1 Public Service Broadcasting: By now, mass media had become a prime mover in social development. Both print and broadcast media emerged as important sources of information which was thought to be the missing link in the development chain. The state-controlled mass media channels and institutions in majority of developing countries were entrusted with the task of information dissemination in what is known as public service broadcasting or PSB.

The public service broadcasting, as a distinct genre of broadcasting, originated in Europe in the 1920s. It was the outcome of the European nations' rejection of both the unregulated, free market model developing in the United States as well as the directly regulated, state-controlled system emerging in the Soviet Union. As a result, a variety of public service broadcasting systems developed across the continent. However, this particular model of public service broadcasting gained currency and was developed in many other countries across the world, including many decolonized nations of Asia, Africa and Latin America in the 1950s and 1960s.

"The goals of public service broadcasting vary from country to country and changed over time. Associated as the first Director General of the BBC, John Reith opined, public service broadcasting basically regards information as a social good not a commodity. Broadcasting serves the community not the market. Several principles are seen as providing the foundations on which public service broadcasting operates. As a valuable public property the government should regulate—but not directly run—broadcasting to maintain standards and diversity of programming. It should be financed through public funds such as the licence fee to guarantee its independence of the market and the pressure of making a profit. It should serve the interests of the nation, and not any particular social group or vested interest. Broadcasters should be politically and publicly accountable. The broadcasting service should be universal and everyone should be able to have access to it", Williams wrote while discussing the theoretical underpinnings of PSB. [19]

In the light of these goals, the mass media can only be socially responsible, politically independent and publicly accountable through public service. However, according to critics, the public service broadcasters have not always discharged their responsibilities effectively. Instead of expanding the public sphere by giving voice to diverse viewpoints, these broadcasters have been reduced to government mouthpieces with no room for political debate and democratic accountability. Rather than giving correct and factual news, exposing political wrong-doings, corruptions and scams, they are made to serve the vested interests of their political masters whose lack of commitment, not of financial resources, is often the real cause of human neglect. [20] This is why despite efforts to make public service broadcasting autonomous by readjusting their institutional and broadcasting structures and output, PSB has failed to realize its full potential in many developing countries, including India.

4.9 The Two-Step Flow

However, a contrarian view regarding the all pervasive power and influence of the mass media came to light during a voter study on the US presidential election. The findings of the research study entitled 'The People's Choice' by Paul Lazarsfeld and others into the impact of mass media on peoples' voting behaviour in the US Presidential election in 1949 virtually demolished the hypodermic needle theory about mass media effects. [21] It, thus, ended the notion of an all-powerful media.

The study, among other things, highlighted the role of factors other than the mass media in political decision-making. It showed how personal influence is more significant in changing people's opinions than the all-pervasive media blizzard. It also showed how some people are more influential than others. Known as opinion leaders, these are people who, on account of their knowledge and views as well as experience and practical wisdom, are well respected in their communities and societies. They often have strong political beliefs and pay close attention to media content. Yet, they are less likely to be influenced by it although they spend more than average time in consuming the media. This is due to their strong belief system in a particular matter. And, whatever they learn from the media, they transmit it to others through personal contacts. They are held in high esteem in their social milieu.

Thus, the voter study revealed limited effects of the mass media. It proved the point held by many that the influence of mass media, if it had any, was confined to reinforcing the existing attitudes and opinions. It also highlighted the pluralistic role of society by identifying the role played by opinion leaders in decision-making. These opinion leaders came from all walks of life and need not have high status or economic advantage over others. Yet, they wielded considerable influence in moulding and mobilizing public opinion in more ways than one.

The conclusive inferences drawn from the study also showed that the mass media effects were neither direct nor as powerful as it was assumed to be. It thus exposed the weakness of the mass media in directly influencing personal choices of the individuals. These findings led to the two-step flow theory of mass media communication effects. The first step here was from the mass media to opinion leaders, while the second step was from these leaders to others in the community.

Thus, the two-step model emphasized the minimal or limited part played by the media in influencing and shaping an individual's decisions about the choices they make in elections or everyday life.

This view was further reinforced by another seminal study on the influence and power of the mass media by social scientist Carl Hovland in 1953. His research on the war propaganda films showed how the mass media were ineffective in improving attitudes of soldiers towards their allies and increasing motivation to fight. Together, these two research studies completely nailed the reigning theory of the day regarding the direct, uniform and all powerful effects of mass media.

4.10 Uses and Gratifications Approach

The two-step flow model led to a more complex understanding of media effects. Media research and theory began to focus on audience to explain the ways in which people select, reject and assess media information. It centred on three key areas of study namely:

- **Selective Exposure:** How and why people chose to selectively expose themselves to media content;
- **Selective Perception:** How audience chose to retain and reject some messages while others are rejected; and
- **Selective Retention:** How and why certain messages are retained by the audience while the others are not.

The research findings proved that the mass media audience was no longer a dumb and passive audience of the war years. Rather, it was intelligent and clever enough to accept or reject a media message. This understanding shifted the focus from what the media do to people to what people do with the media. The resultant uses and gratification approach on media effects assumed that the audience brought their own needs and desires to the process of making sense of media messages. Needs and desires determined the way messages are received and understood by the audience. According to Katz, "such an approach assumes that even the most potent of mass media content cannot ordinarily influence an individual who has no 'use' of it in the social and psychological context in which he lives. The 'uses' approach assumes that people's values, their interests, their associations, their social roles, are pre-potent and that people selectively fashion what they see and hear to these interests. [22]

Thus, media filled an important social need. This point

was well made in Herzog's [23] study of women's consumption of radio soaps in 1944. The study showed as to how radio soaps served a number of functions other than information, education and entertainment in women's lives. The radio soaps fulfilled an important social need by providing emotional release and serving as a source of information and advice to make sense of the world. Clearly, the radio had successfully positioned itself as a reliable source of popular entertainment and information. Truly, the days of thick unending Victorian novels as an emotional succour during long winter evenings were well nigh over for women.

Almost three decades later in 1972, McQuail, Blumler and Brown made a similar point when they said that mass media fulfilled the social need some people have for companionship. By examining five types of programmes—a radio serial, from television, a soap, a quiz show, the news and two adventure series—they concluded there were four types of uses and gratifications such as: [24]

1. **Diversion:** The media provides diversion in different ways. They allow people to escape from the constraints of routine that make up everyday life. They can help people to escape from their worries and personal problems, and they can provide emotional release.
2. **Personal Relationships:** The media provides personal relationships for some people in the form of companionship. It is argued that 'the characters may become virtually real, knowable and cherished individuals, and their voices are more than just a comforting background which breaks the silence of an empty house'. [25] The content of the media can also be used as a source of conversational material in people's lives i.e. it serves as social utility for viewers and listeners.
3. **Personal Identity:** They can act as points of personal reference for individuals, to reflect on aspects of their own lives or personal situations. The content of programmes can provide people with information to develop ideas

about the problems they are facing in their lives—a process of reality exploration—as well as reinforce their views and values.

4. **Surveillance:** The media offers the opportunity for surveillance of what is going on in the world, to keep abreast of issues and events.

4.10.1 Entertainment-Education Approach: Despite significant differences between the dominant and dependency theories of development, the role of communication within the two paradigms strongly recommended the use of communication methods and media products to persuade audience to change. This led to the formulation of an 'entertainment-education' strategy based on the uses and gratification theory of mass media effects. Pioneered by Miguel Sabido, a renowned television producer-director of Mexico in the 1960s, it entailed purposely designing and implementing media message to both entertain and educate the audience. It aimed at imparting knowledge about an educational issue, creating favourable attitudes and changing overt behaviour.

This approach sought to capitalize on the popular appeal of the entertainment media through radio and television to show individuals how they can live safer, healthier and happier lives. Many developing countries including India, Mexico, Brazil, South Korea, Pakistan and Turkey adopted this technique to raise awareness about social issues and bring about desired attitudinal and behavioural changes through their social messages.

In India, it began with the broadcasting of television serial 'Hum Log' (We the People) in 1984-85. Its broadcast was not only a turning point in the growth and expansion of television in the country but also in the field of television entertainment. It was India's first long-running soap opera which utilized the entertainment-education strategy by meticulously placing educational and social message in its entertainment quotient. 'Hum Log' achieved audience ratings of 65 to 90 percent in North India and between 20 to 45 percent in main Southern

Indian cities. About 50 million individuals watched the average broadcast of 'Hum Log'. Its producers received over 400,000 letters from viewers in response to the serial.

'Hum Log' was followed by 'Buniyaad' (Foundation) based on the theme of partition of India into Hindusthan and Pakistan in 1947. It was followed by Ramayana in 1987. It attracted smash ratings that could only be outnumbered by phenomenally successful Mahabharat in 1988-89. Their respective producers, late Ramanand Sagar and late B. R. Chopra did a great service not only to the Indian audience but also to the entire humanity by spreading the universally relevant messages of these two great Indian epics.

This strategy is still relevant and very much in use. In Turkey, for instance, a serial named 'Fatmagul" was telecast to raise awareness about the evil of rape and its ill effects. It is a touching story of a village damsel by the name Fatmagul who is gang-raped and abandoned by her fiancé. Traumatized Fatmagul slowly recovers with the help of family and friends and finally stands vindicated in her fight against the perpetrators of this heinous crime. The rapists are punished, their families are ostracized and Fatmagul emerges victorious in her valiant struggle. The serial highlights the effective criminal justice system, the broad social support extended to the victim and above all, the painstaking efforts made by the protagonist to retrieve her dignity and personal image. The serial was a smashing hit and broke all TRP records in Turkey. It was subsequently telecast in many other countries including India. One wonders as to why no such serial has been made in India which, of late, has become infamous for rapes the world over.

AIR: Likewise, the All India Radio (AIR) adopted various entertainment formats, such as soap operas, variety programmes, interactive talk shows, and features to engage audiences while educating them simultaneously. For instance, a 13-episode radio series entitled 'Jeevan Saurabh' (Fragrance of Life) and 'Jeevan Saurabh II' broadcast in 1988, broke new grounds by addressing the sensitive issue of adolescence and related problems like teenage sexuality, intergenerational conflicts and career choices. It was a trendsetter and pioneered the concept of long-running entertainment-education radio serials such as 'Dehleez', 'Tinka Tinka Sukh' and 'Yeh Kahan Aa Gaye Hum'. These programmes were designed on the basis of a prior audience needs' assessment, and employed a team of writers and subject matter specialists. Pre-programme publicity employing a variety of mass media, including the vernacular press, was also done.

Also, various techniques were employed to enhance the 'interactivity' of the radio programmes with target audience members. Thousands of listeners were encouraged to register to listen to these radio serials in advance of their broadcasts assuring an audience for them when the broadcasts began. These registered listeners were also encouraged to write letters in response to the various social issues raised in these radio serials. These letters were then discussed in specific listener interaction programmes, and prizes were awarded for viewer's response. [26]

The impact of these radio serials, originally produced in national language Hindi, was multiplied through the process of their transcreation, which involves adapting an existing serial's plot, characters and context to suit the needs of another audience. For instance, the Hindi version of 'Tinka Tinka Sukh' was transcreated in four other languages of the Southern Indian states. Its plot, characters and context were suitably modified to incorporate the intended social message.

4.11 Participatory Approach to Communication

The decade of the 1980s was a time for stock taking. It was a time when the promises of the modernization had failed to materialize and the dependency theorists too had fallen short of providing a successful alternative model of development. Scholars and administrators were busy reviewing communication for development theory, development projects and information programmes to assess their contribution, or lack of it, to the overall development scenario in the developing world.

Amidst all this confusion, a different approach focusing on people's participation began to emerge. Known as 'Another Development', this participatory model considered participation to be an integral part of development process. It was less oriented towards the political-economic dimension and more rooted in the cultural realities of development. It shifted its focus from economic growth to social dimensions of development and emphasized sustainability and people's participation as envisaged in the Millennium Development Goals or MDGs. According to the World Bank, "Internationally, emphasis is being placed on the challenge of sustainable development, and participation is increasingly recognized as a necessary part of sustainable development strategies".

The communication approach in participatory paradigm was aimed at facilitating capacity building and empowerment. It discarded the top-down, one-way flow of communication rooted in the modernization paradigm in favour of a more dialogic and two-way conception of communication. The two-way model promoted people's active and direct interaction through consultation and dialogue over the traditional one-way information dissemination through mass media. Even mass media messages, in this approach, tend to originate from people themselves rather than from 'outside experts' as in the case of community radio.

4.11.1 Community Radio: Since its invention in 1901 by Marconi, radio has been very useful in information dissemination both for propaganda and mass mobilization. Its subsequent avatar, the inexpensive battery-powered transistor radio, has proved to be a highly effective medium for social good in the developing world as it has broad coverage and transcends the illiteracy barrier. No less than 85 percent of the world's population today is within the easy reach of radio broadcasts that play a significant role in participatory approach to development communication.

Community radio, as the name suggests, is owned, managed and accountable to a community. The community can be either based on geographical location or commonality of interests and aspirations. Communities can be large, if the concerned stakeholders cover several local districts, or small areas, such as a village or a group, in a large city or remote rural area. Community radio enhances civic engagement in poor and marginalized communities. It is highly effective in magnifying the impacts of development initiatives by involving and engaging local listeners in the process.

Community broadcasting can help social groups living in remote communities and facing linguistic, ethnic and literacy barriers to articulate priority issues and problems. For instance, by discussing sensitive issues like domestic violence, drug abuse and sexually transmitted diseases, the community radio gives listeners access to subjects that might not be otherwise addressed by the community or discussed in individual households. Such informed discussions can significantly affect individual and group behaviour and improve the ability of community members to raise and analyze problems and work together to solve them.

The community radio station is not run for profit but is free to mobilize resources to meet its operational costs. Its governance structure is designed to promote transparency and independence to ensure it remains responsive to community needs and aspirations. It has proven to be a sustainable medium for poor and marginalized populations to be heard and informed, shape knowledgeable opinions, learn the give-and-take of informed dialogue so as to become decisive agents in their own development through participation.

Given its growing recognition as an important part of a diverse and pluralistic media landscape, many developing countries like India and Nepal have developed appropriate legal and regulatory frameworks to ensure good practices in their broadcast policies that recognize and differentiate between public service, private commercial and non-profit community broadcasting. Consequently, community radio has emerged as one of the key components of rural communication.

4.11.2 The Role of Culture: The role of culture in development and social change is integral to participatory approach to communication which recognizes that local cultures, contrary to modernization perspective, are dynamic and not static and therefore continuously changing. Hence, the interaction between local culture and other elements in a society undergoing change is dynamic and therefore progressive. [27] Culture therefore is an effective facilitator of development and not otherwise.

This shift towards culture has brought various indigenous channels of communication into limelight. These cultural channels, collectively called the folk media, have incorporated various concepts of participatory development such as self-reliance, capacity-building and empowerment. As products of the local culture, the folk media are rich in cultural symbols, intimate with the people at the grassroots and highly participatory in approach. These features help them to integrate with the modern mass media as in the case of community radio.

4.11.3 The Folk Media: Rooted in the concept of 'Sadharanikaran', the Indian concept of communications, various folk or traditional art forms like *keertan, the jatra, tamasha* and *alha* have been employed since yore for moral teachings and creating socio-political awareness through entertainment. For instance, the Sannyasi Revolt against the British in Bengal was spread by folk singers known as 'Bowls'. Later, a film called 'Anand Math' with 'Vande Mataram' as its signature song was made on this uprising. Thus, the folk media are personal, familiar and more credible forms of communication especially in rural areas. Their audience, irrespective of their literacy levels, can easily identify with their format and contents as 'sahridayas'.

Scholars and intellectuals have seen certain advantages in these folk art forms or folk media that could be exploited for development purposes such as: [28]

1. Personal Appeal: Being close to the hearts and minds of the people, their appeal can be at a personal and intimate level. Further, their familiar format and content, as also colloquial dialects facilitate clarity in communication.
2. Instant Rapport: No cross-cultural communication hurdles are encountered here. The numerous and different forms available for specific homogenous groups and for specific purposes can be exploited to cater to people of different regions, on home ground as it were. Rapport is immediate and direct; the barriers to communication are almost non-existent. They are available to all and sundry, and enjoyed by persons of different age groups—at a very low cost.
3. Flexibility: The greatest advantage of the folk forms over the electronic media is their flexibility in accommodating new themes. Comments on current events are introduced in the traditional form of *tamasha* or the *jatra* or even the *keertan*. These are hardly ever interpreted as interpolations as the folk media are not 'pure' forms. Indian folk forms are not rigid and have a generous mix of dialogue, dance, song, clowning, moralizing and prayer.
4. Lasting Impact: Unlike electronic media, various folk forms cater to small audiences on which they can leave lasting impact. The audiences' deep involvement results in voluntarily participation in *keertan, alha* and other street theatre genres.
5. Self-expression: The folk art forms satisfy our innate need for self-expression, for moral instruction combined with entertainment, and for the dramatic and the lyrical. The folk media preserve and disseminate in a lively manner, the tradition and culture of our forefathers.

Thus, with its emphasis on culture and traditional art forms, the communication approach in participative paradigm helped in the development of a community's cultural identity. The renewed folk art forms acted as vehicles for citizen's self-expression. They facilitated problem articulation and served as tools for the diagnosis of community's problems. Even today, the folk media play an important role in rural communication for development and social change.

4.12 Expansion of Public Sphere

By shifting the emphasis from information dissemination to situation analysis, from media to people and persuasion to participation, the new paradigm changed the way communication is conceived and applied. This is evident from the new definition of development communication as "a social process based on dialogue using a broad range of tools and methods. It is also about seeking change at different levels, including listening, building trust, sharing knowledge and skills, building policies, debating, and learning for sustained and meaningful change". [29] Here, dialogue is the key element in building trust, sharing knowledge and ensuring mutual understanding. This conception of development communication, unlike the top-down PSB model, has led to the expansion of public sphere by advocating a systematic use of communication to involve and inform people in the planning and implementation of development projects.

Hence, the participatory approach to communication can also be called 'communication for social change' as it is anchored in the philosophy of knowledge-sharing and learning among all stakeholders involved in development. It sees people as the nucleus of change and emphasizes the importance of two-way communication to facilitate stakeholders' participation and empowerment in the development process. Moreover, it seeks social change with the people and not for the people. This approach not only reduces political risks but also improves project design and performance. It increases transparency of activities by enhancing people's voices and participation.

By giving voice to the voiceless, the participatory approach to development has immensely helped in the expansion of the public sphere. This expansion has led to greater participation and therefore greater transparency in decision-making in development initiatives. It has, thus, tried to answer the call for democratization of communication by the MacBride Commission appointed for the Study of Communication Problems. Its chairman, Sean MacBride had called "for a new attitude for overcoming stereotyped thinking and to promote more understanding of diversity and plurality, with full respect for the dignity and equality of peoples living in different conditions and acting in different ways". [30] In this respect, the role of participatory approach to development in democratizing communication is in tandem with that of the new media powered by highly advanced information and communications technologies or ICTs.

4.12.1 Facilitating Participation through New Technologies: The emergence of new media and the spread of internet over the past decade have facilitated the rise of new forms of civil participation. These include e-governance, online petitions, mass demonstrations, crowd-funding and blogging. Although petitions, protests, fundraising and political publications have long existed, the internet has allowed them to achieve unprecedented coverage, bringing people together across physical borders with enormous speed.

Activists can now gather support from millions of people in a few weeks and with limited resources, permitting them to have an impact on public and political life that would have been impossible through traditional means of participation. This has challenged government and party monopolies in politics and effectively broadened civil participation. New technologies have also helped previously excluded groups—such as people with limited mobility, people living in secluded areas and young people—participate in public and political life. [31]

Thus, given its enormous developmental potential, the participatory approach to communication need to pay close attention to the following considerations such as: [32]

1. Communication as a basic human need: The satisfaction of the need for communication is just as important for a society as the concern for health, nutrition, housing, education and labour. Together with all the other social needs, communication must enable the citizens to emancipate

themselves completely. The right to inform and to be informed, and the right to communicate, are thus essential human rights both individually and collectively.

2. Communication is a facet of social conscientization, emancipation and liberation process: The social responsibility of the media in the process of social change is very large. Indeed, after the period of formal education, the media is the most important educational and socializing agent. They are capable of informing or disinforming, exposing or concealing important facts, interpreting events positively or negatively, and so on.
3. Communication task involves rights and responsibilities and obligations. Since the media provide a public service, they must carry it out in a framework of social and judicial responsibility that reflects the social consensus of the society. In other words, there are no rights without obligations.

Endnotes

1. McQuail, Denis (1979), "Towards a Sociology of Communication".
2. Tiwari, I.P. (1980), "Sadharanikaran: Indian Communication Theory", *Indian and Foreign Review*, June.
3. McQuail, Denis (1994), "Mass Communication Theory: An Introduction", London: Sage Publications.
4. Quebral, Nora, 1975.
5. Lerner, Daniel (1958), "The Passing of Traditional Society".
6. Katz, Elihu, and Paul F. Lazarsfeld (1955), "Personal Influence: The Part Played by People in the Flow of Mass Communications", New York: Free Press.
7. Rogers, Everett M. (1983), "Diffusion of Innovation", New York: The Free Press, p. 5.
8. Ibid.
9. Kotler, P. (1975), "Marketing for Non-profit Organizations", New Jersey: Prentice Hall.
10. Ibid.
11. Lazarsfeld, Paul F. and Robert K. Merton (1964), "Friendship as a Social Process: A Substantive and Methodological Analysis", in Monroe Berger and others (eds.), 'Freedom and Control in a Modern Society', New York: Octagon.

12. Copp, James H. et al. (1958), "The Function of Information Sources in the Farm Practice Adoption Process", Rural Sociology in Rogers, 1983.
13. Rogers and Shoemaker, 1971.
14. Ibid.
15. Schramm, Wilbur (1964), "Mass Media and National Development", California: Stanford University Press.
16. Ibid.
17. Hale, J. (1975), "Radio Power: Propaganda and International Broadcasting", London: Paul Elek.
18. Lasswell, Harold (1948), "The Structure and Function of Communication in Society", in Lyman Bryson (ed.), 'The Communication of Ideas', New York: Harper and Brothers.
19. Williams, Kevin (2003), "Understanding Media Theory", London: Arnold.
20. UNDP, 1991.
21. Lazarsfeld, P., B. Berelson and H. Gaudet (1948), "The People's Choice", New York: Columbia Press.
22. Katz, E. (1959), "Mass Communication Research and the Study of Culture in Studies in Public Communication".
23. Herzog, H. (1944), "What Do We Really Know About Day-time Serial Listeners?", in Lazarsfeld, P. (ed.), 'Radio Research', New York: Duell, Sloan and Pearce.
24. McQuail et al. (1972).
25. Ibid.
26. Singhal, Arvind and Everett M. Rogers (2001), "India's Communication Revolution", New Delhi: Sage Publications.
27. Dissanayake, W. (1984), "A Buddhist Approach to Development: A Sri Lankan Endeavour", in G. Wang and W. Dissanayake (eds.), 'Continuity and Change in Communication Systems', New Jersey: Ablex.
28. Melkote.
29. First World Congress of Communication for Development, Rome, 2006.
30. MacBride Commission Report (1983), UNESCO.
31. Human Development Report Office.
32. Somavia, Juan as quoted in Servaes, Jan and Malikhao Patchanee (2005), 'Media and Global Change: Rethinking Communication for Development', Buenos Aires: Clasco.

5

The Road Ahead

Many problems and challenges of underdevelopment that existed at the time of decolonization continue to persist even today. Rather some of them like uncontrolled population, poverty, inequality, unemployment and environmental degradation have assumed gigantic proportions. These challenges have become further complicated by lingering disparities like ever-widening gulf between the rich and the poor, deepening inequalities in income and emerging challenges such as growing threat of pan-Islamist radicalism and violent extremism to the entire humanity. The situation is particularly grave for countries like India which is a victim of relentless proxy war and terrorism exported from Pakistan, the epicentre of Islamist radicalism in the world.

5.1 Demographic Explosion

According to noted historian Eric Hobsbawm, population explosion is the central fact of Third World's existence. However, the important thing is not the number of states, 'but the enormous and growing demographic weight and pressure they represented collectively'. [1]

"This demographic explosion in the poor countries of the world, which first caused serious international worry, is probably the most fundamental change in the Short Twentieth Century…A world population that doubled in the forty years since 1950, or a population like that of Africa which can expect to double in less than thirty years, is entirely without historical precedent, as are the practical problems it must raise. One has merely to consider the social and economic situation of a country 60 percent of whose people are less than fifteen years old". [2]

Even today, the astonishing demographic explosion in this

part of the world continues to change the balance of world population which is projected to grow to staggering 9.7 billion by 2050. [3] In 2000, there were about 1.3 billion poor in the developing countries and now this figure is expected to rise to 1.5 billion by 2025 with Asia and Africa having the largest concentration of the world's poor. This situation is putting an enormous burden on the world economy as tens and thousands of additional mouths are needed to be fed every year. Population growth is therefore inversely proportional to economic growth. This is particularly true of developing countries like India where no concerted effort has been made to mitigate the situation.

Though both China and India had, in their wisdom, tried to control their giant populations through 'one-child policy and sterilization programme of the 1970s respectively, the former succeeded while the later failed. The communist China's success in this regard was due to its strong iron fist authoritarian style of functioning; whereas democratic and secular India's poor performance was squarely attributed to its vote bank politics and communal policy of minority appeasement at the cost of wider national interests. Consequently, India has miserably lagged behind China be it human resource development or infrastructure development. For instance, of the 73 roads expected to be constructed along the Indo-China border by 2012-13, only 30 have been completed. Reasons for delay, according to a written reply by the Home Ministry to a parliamentary query, are: limited work season, logistical issues due to high altitude and difficult terrain, delay in forest nods and land acquisition. [4]

Now compare this with rapacious China that after forcibly annexing Tibet and defeating India in 1962 war has created a wide network of roads and railroads up to Sikkim including the strategic Karakoram Highway to encircle India in vulnerable North and North-East including the Middle Sector. It also controls a part of POK territory and has built ports in Balochistan and Sri Lanka. It is a well known fact that expansionist China has a keen propensity to foment trouble be it India, Bhutan or the South China Sea. It enjoys a considerable hold over Nepal, Myanmar and Bangladesh from where arms and ammunition are supplied to secessionist elements like the radical Islamists and naxalites waging a relentless war against the Indian State.

All this is a result of India's glaring failure in harnessing its bloating population 65 percent of which is less than 35 years of age. Due to its dangerous appeasement politics, a particular section of society continues to languish in an area of darkness as it is exempted from the family planning norms under which a limit of two children has been fixed for all government servants. It is the same section that displays sharp inequality in income. While majority is poor and backward on account of its growing population in the name of religion, a small section is extremely rich and polygamous. Worse still, the situation has become a severe threat to country's safety and security as it is being readily exploited by radical and extremist elements to destabilize India. They particularly target the population of denationalized and radicalized youth who are quite vulnerable to the nefarious influence of anti-national and fissiparous elements as was evident during the recent communal flare up in Bengal's Basirhaat.

This situation has an adverse impact on all development initiatives as every genuine and sincere effort at rebuilding India is either derailed by loot, plunder and arson as is happening in Kashmir valley where the security forces are targeted with stones, petrol and acid bombs while schools and police stations are burnt; or tends to fall short of expectations of the ever growing population. However, a majority of sensible people, irrespective of caste or creed, understand the importance of family planning in national life and readily adopt the two-child norm. India, therefore, urgently needs a national policy on population control for safety, security and sustainable development of the country in the tumultuous 21st century.

5.2 Tackling Poverty

It is both a cause as well as an outcome of uncontrolled population. In a way, poverty is directly proportional to population explosion that leads to further squeeze in income. This vicious circle creates a particular mindset as in the words of Hobsbawm: "Most Asian and Islamic peasants were much poorer, or at least worse fed—sometimes, as in India, desperately and historically poor—and the pressure of men and women on limited lands, was already more severe. Nevertheless, it seemed to many of them that the best solution to their problems was not to get involved with those who told them that economic development would bring untold wealth and prosperity, but to keep them at bay. Long experience had shown them and their ancestors before them, that no good came from outside. Generations of silent calculation had taught them that minimizing risks was a better policy than maximizing profits". [5]

This aforementioned propensity to minimize risk, a typical characteristic of the rural poor, is described as 'the subculture of peasantry' by eminent social scientist and scholar Everett M. Rogers. This resistance to change and modernization has adversely affected the economic growth thereby further widening the gulf between the rich and the poor. It is generally seen that population growth is usually fastest where poverty is greatest and health and education services are weakest as in the rural areas of the least developed countries. As a result, the percentage of world population that experienced negative growth in the 1980s was four times the percentage in the 1970s. Of these, more than 60 percent had, during the same period, experienced growth rates of three percent or more. [6] And, despite consistent efforts at reducing poverty in the last 25 years, nearly 786 million people, with 385 million of them being children, lived on less than US$ 1.90 a day in 2013. [7] This further proves the point that uncontrolled population is the root cause of all man-made problems, including poverty and environment degradation, facing the world today.

Poverty often gets manifested in more than one way. There are many dimensions to it apart from low and meagre income and inability to meet one's basic needs. According to multidimensional poverty index (MPI), deprived people often lack capabilities and opportunities across multiple dimensions. Almost 1.2 billion people in the developing countries live in multidimensional poverty, 53.9 percent of them in South Asia and 33.5 percent in Sub-Saharan Africa. [8]

Experts have inferred some systematic patterns of deprivation from poverty measures. Nearly half of people in rural areas worldwide lack access to improved sanitation facilities, compared with a sixth of people in urban areas. Likewise, twice as many rural children as urban children are out of school. So also the slum dwellers, accounting for 48 percent of the urban population in developing countries, are deprived of those very services and opportunities for which they migrated from rural areas. Thus, a far greater proportion of people are poor in rural areas than in urban areas, and in urban areas poor people are often clustered in slums. Consequently, more than a billion people live in housing that is below minimum standards of comfort and sanitation.

Regional disparities between and within countries also account for uneven distribution of opportunities and services. They can directly affect the ability to access health care, education, water and housing as also the quality of services that can greatly vary within regions in a country. For instance, a comparative study of the two states of Kerala and Uttar Pradesh in India, in the mid-2000s, vividly highlighted this difference. While Kerala had one public hospital bed per 1,299 people, Uttar Pradesh had only one bed per 20,041 people. This inequality in health care was further evident from the fact that almost all births in Kerala were attended by health personnel, compared with just 27 percent in Uttar Pradesh. [9]

Likewise, people in conflict zones and conflict-affected countries are at a much greater risk of falling into multidimensional poverty trap as conflict limits the availability of essential services like nutrition, health care and education. Livelihoods are similarly affected when violence and extremism interferes with trade, infrastructure and service provision. Same is true of migrants and refugees. The plight of displaced Hindu refugees from Pakistan, seeking security and shelter in India, is no different from that of millions of Kashmiri Hindu migrants, the original inhabitants of Kashmir, thrown out their hearths and homes in the wake of ethnic cleansing by radical Islamist zealots and pro-Pakistan separatists in the valley. Named after Rishi Kashyap, Kashmir was originally known as 'Kashyap Marg' and was renowned as the seat of Sanskrit learning and Shaivism.

5.3 Problem of Inequalities

Poverty invariably leads to inequality. It gets manifested in income inequality between regions and within countries. Income inequality creates gulf between the rich and the poor. This gulf further translates into rural-urban divide and has a significant impact on social life in the form of gender bias with women at the receiving end.

5.3.1 Income inequality: It is reflected worldwide particularly in the gap in per capita GNP between the developed North or members of the Organisation for Economic Cooperation and Development (OECD) and the backward South comprising 'low and middle economies' of Asia, Africa and Latin America. Consequently, in 1970, the first group averaged 14.5 times the GNP per capita of the second but over 24 times the poor countries' GNP per capita in 1990. Similar trend was reflected in the global distribution of income as well. From 1965 to 1980, nearly 77 percent of the world's population earned about 15 percent of its income. Expressed in GNP per capita, the average income in the North (US$ 12,510) was 18 times the average in the South (US$ 710).

Unmindful of this widening gulf, the Third World underestimated the constraints of backwardness. "They lacked skilled and experienced experts, administrators and economic cadres; illiteracy; unfamiliarity or lack of sympathy with programmes of economic modernization—especially when their governments set themselves targets which even developed countries found difficult, such as centrally state-planned industrialization. Ghana, with Sudan the first sub-Saharan African state to be granted independence, thus threw away currency reserves of two hundred million, accumulated thanks to high cocoa prices and wartime earnings—higher than the sterling balances of independent India—in an attempt to build an industrialized state-controlled economy…The results were disastrous, and made worse by the collapse of cocoa prices in the 1960s", notes Hobsbawm. [10]

Further, inequalities in income led to inequalities in other dimension of well-being and vice versa. According to UNDP, as of now, the top one percent of the global wealth distribution holds 46 percent of the world's wealth. This inequality in income leaves the excluded groups voiceless as they have little political leverage to influence policy and legislation through traditional means. In a way, it is a continuation of the old debate on whether trade increases all-round prosperity or has the effect of widening the economic gap.

However, income inequality within regions is merely a tip of the iceberg. Hidden beneath are the lingering disparities within countries as national income figures can only broadly indicate the distribution of poverty in a country. They do not reveal the deep and persistent inequalities between the rich and the poor, men and women, and urban and rural divide. It, therefore, needs an incisive scrutiny into the system to understand the ever-widening gulf between the rich and poor so markedly evident in their respective lifestyles, life expectancy, food and nutrition, education, healthcare and employment opportunities.

While the rich every here can afford the best that life can offer, the poor, with their meagre income, can barely manage to eke out a living. They fail to meet their basic needs like food, clothing and shelter. As a result, life expectancy nay human survival gets compromised. Lack of adequate nutrition and healthcare increases the risk of infant and maternal mortality. Education too varies with income. Non-availability of schools and financial support kills any incentive for education among the poorest of the poor.

5.3.2 Gender Inequality: It gets manifested in gender bias that works in favour of men as against women. This inequality between men and women further worsens the condition of socio-economic deprivation. Deprived of education, women are confined to the household chores. Girl child is either not encouraged to enrol in school or is compelled to make an early exit. This explains the alarming drop out rate among girl children. Not so long ago, in South Asia alone, the female literacy rates were only half those of males—as in Afghanistan (24 percent), Sudan (2.5 percent) and Sierra Leone (30 percent).

A. Female Foeticide: The worst manifestation of gender bias is the practice of female foeticide in which, after sex determination, a female foetus is killed inside the womb itself. This evil practice, still prevalent in patriarchal societies the world over, is a product of societal preference for males over females. For instance, according to 2011 Census figures, the child sex ratio (0-6 years) in India is one of the poorest with 918 girls for 1,000 boys. This bias against the girl child is evident in the significant drop in female ratio per 1,000 males. As per 2011 Census, the number of females per 1,000 males averaged around 943. However, this was a marked improvement over the Census figures of 2001 that showed 933 females per 1,000 males.

B. Low Female Sex Ratio: Despite stringent punitive measures to curb female foeticide and encourage social acceptance of a girl child through aggressive social marketing of pro-girl schemes like *Beti Bachao, Beti Padhao* (Save girl child, educate girl child), the situation is far from satisfactory. There are states where sex ratio is even less than 900 per 1,000 males such as Delhi with 866 females; Haryana—877 females, Jammu and Kashmir—883 females, Sikkim—889 females while Punjab has 893 females per 1,000 males. The condition is no better in Union Territories with Chandigarh having 818 females per 1,000 males; Dadra and Nagar Haveli—775 females per 1,000 males and Daman and Diu lagging behind with 618 females per 1,000 males.

The situation is equally pathetic in states like Uttar Pradesh with 908 females per 1,000 males; Bihar with 916 females per 1,000 males and Gujarat with 918 females per 1,000 males. Both Maharashtra and Rajasthan respectively have 925 and 926 females per 1,000 males while Madhya Pradesh and Nagaland fare slightly better with 930 and 931 females per 1,000 males respectively. The two states that have done exceedingly well are Kerala, famous for its matriarchal society, with 1,084 females per 1,000 males and Puducherry with 1,038 females per 1,000 males.

C. Crimes against Women: According to National Crimes Records Bureau (NCRB), nearly 3.27 lakh cases of crimes against women were reported across the country in 2015. Of these, over 1.3 lakh were sexual offences—1.2 lakh in states and 9,445 in union territories. The sexual offence cases included rape, attempt to commit rape, assault on women with intent to outrage her modesty and insult to modesty of women.

Interestingly, the states and union territories with lowest sex ratios like Delhi have the highest incidence of crimes against women. In 2015 alone, over 34,600 cases of rapes were reported across the country with Madhya Pradesh and Delhi topping the infamous list of states and union territories. Of these, in 33,098 cases, the offenders were known to the victims. The rape victims were among the age group of below six years to over 60 years. Madhya Pradesh had reported 4,391 rape cases, the highest among the states, whereas Delhi, notorious for its Nirbhaya case, had reported 2,199 such cases.

The growing incidence of rapes and other sex crimes against women point to moral depravity that has set in the

Indian society. This downturn cannot be arrested by law or other such measures. How else could one explain the continuous violation and abuse of minor girls, infants and toddlers, leave aside saree-clad women in their 70s, by men of all ages, including adolescents, on an every day basis. While some blame it to repressive and conservative social mentality, the others to cultural transition, Western influence and social networking sites. Whatever be the reason, the growing incidence of rapes and other sex crimes portray a very negative picture of the country as a whole.

The answer to this problem, according to one point of view, lies not in logic but in ancient wisdom and yoga that teaches mental discipline and self-control. It is argued that the common man in India has been traditionally God-fearing, hard working and generally truthful. Women have been well-respected and cared for. Therefore, this moral turpitude, which is alien to Indian culture and ethos, has not come in a day or two. Rather, it has been systematically and in a planned way injected into the system to distract people from the path of truth (satya) and dharma (righteous conduct) by the corrupt at high places during the 70-odd years of India's existence as an independent country. After all, 'yatha raja, tatha praja' i.e. as the king, so the subject be!

D. Human Trafficking: Low female ratio often results in unavailability of young women for marriage purposes. The shortage of brides indirectly encourages human trafficking. For instance, young marriageable girls from poor households in Jharkhand and Odisha are readily sold for a price in states like Punjab and Haryana. Once purchased at an appropriate 'bride price', these girls spend their lives as bonded labourers and are denied their rightful place in the family.

The role of Indian media in highlighting the issue has been praiseworthy. In particular, Sony channel's TV show 'Crime Patrol' based on true stories picked up from police records, have shown horrifying real life accounts of poor young hapless women trapped in fake marriages and working as bonded labourers in states with low or very low female ratio.

E. Misuse of Law: Gender inequality is often enforced by negative use of law as happened in the infamous Shah Bano case, a controversial maintenance lawsuit in India way back in 1985. In this case, the Supreme Court judgement favouring maintenance through alimony to Shah Bano, a 62-year-old aggrieved divorced Muslim woman and a mother of five, was overruled by the then Congress government led by Rajiv Gandhi. Consequently, the Indian Parliament reversed the Supreme Court verdict under pressure from radical Islamists.

Today, one finds the same medieval and regressive mindset behind the denial of women's rights to own or inherit property, to receive pensions or even to decide whether or when to bear children or not. Muslim women in India are still agitating for equal rights within marriage and Muslim community as a whole. Their demand for ending the vicious practice of triple talaq, nikah halala (bar against remarriage with divorced husband without an intervening marriage with another man before getting a divorce from him), and polygamy under Muslim personnel laws is being strongly opposed by Islamist radicals in the name of Sharia or Islamic law that has no locus standi in a secular and democratic country like India whose Constitution is committed to the ideals of justice, liberty and equality, fraternity and freedom of religion. Their opposition in the matter is seen as an effort to thwart the implementation of uniform civil code and end polygamy.

F. Female Genital Mutilation: The barbaric practice of female genital mutilation or FGM, still prevalent in nearly 30 countries of Africa, the Middle East and Asia, constitutes not only the extreme form of discrimination against women but also the most horrifying example of female oppression that reflects deep-rooted inequality between the sexes. Also known as female circumcision, the FMG is a well-entrenched practice in regressive societies where women are considered not more than baby making machines.

The FMG involves a painful procedure that often leads to

death. Like sunnat, it is mostly carried out on minors and is a cruel violation of the rights of children and therefore a gross violation of human rights of girls and women. According to World Health Organisation, the practice also violates a person's right to health, security and physical integrity, the right to be free from torture and cruelty, inhuman or degrading treatment, and the right to life when the life-threatening procedure results in death.

5.3.3 The Rural-Urban Divide: Likewise, the urban-rural divide is manifested in income inequality, lack of employment opportunities and delivery of social services. As majority of the poor live in rural areas, their earnings are much less than those living in towns and cities. This contrast gets further accentuated in the event of agricultural crisis that results in falling incomes from crops, reduced food production and increased malnutrition thereby forcing debt-ridden farmers to commit suicides. The situation is worsened by lack of income generating opportunities.

This glaring disparity leads to imbalance in the delivery of social services. In majority of developing countries, including India, poor are only half as likely to be covered by health services as those in urban areas. The poor do not even get an ambulance to carry the sick or remove the mortal remains of their dear ones while self-serving petty politicians do not mind splurging huge amounts of their ill-gotten wealth on luxury cars and SUVs. A similar contrast is evident in the non-availability of medicines and medical staff to help the needy. Likewise, paucity of safe potable water is another area of concern. Unsafe water makes people unhealthy and sick. No amount of immunization can prevent waterborne diseases and infections if safe drinking water is not available.

So is the sorry state of sanitation with choked and unclean sewage systems that women are compelled to defecate in the open, people littering on the streets with garbage and men spitting at each other. The situation worsens during the monsoon when overflowing ponds and puddles as well as water logging on un-cemented roads turn into breeding factories for dengue and malaria mosquitoes. Educational services too are hit hard by this neglect and apathy towards development which is far less in rural areas. So is the case with employment opportunities which, despite MGNREGA or Mahatma Gandhi National Rural Employment Guarantee Act, are virtually non-existent in rural areas. This invariably leads to migration from rural to urban areas in search of educational and income opportunities.

5.4 Urbanization

In the absence of development, the nexus between growing population and increasing poverty, has led to mass-scale rural migration to urban areas for income generation and employment opportunities. The problem has worsened with the absence of healthcare, nutrition, safe water, education and sanitation in rural areas. Known as urbanization, this trend has become the standard feature of 21st century city life. Cities all over South and South-East Asia are inundated with slums in which over 880 million people, mostly migrants, live. For instance, Mumbai, the financial capital of India, has Dharaavi, the biggest slum in Asia and home to migrants from all over the country. It is the first thing to be noticed dotting the dense landscape of Mumbai as one touches down in the city of Bollywood.

The situation is no better in the national capital where every reasonable colony has an adjoining slum in its backyard. These slums turn into convenient hunting grounds for buying and selling votes during elections. Even historic Connaught Place has not been spared. The mushroom growth of jhuggis or makeshift tenements by migrant labour there has robbed its beauty. The huge amount of money spent on its renovation seems to have gone waste when one looks at the pathetic condition of the once neat and tidy, and now abandoned, underground passage linking the Coffee Home in the Emporia Complex to the ancient Hanuman Mandir on Baba Khadak

Singh Marg in New Delhi. One wonders as to what picture of 'Swach Bharat' is being presented to foreign tourists who frequent it daily for shopping and sight seeing.

Clearly, this fast and furious infestation of urban city centres with slums is the harsh reality of 21st century India that dreams of building brand new smart mega cities but cannot manage its old ones. As per an estimate, nearly 40 percent of the world's future urban expansion may occur in slums or the unplanned cluster of jhuggis. These slums lack adequate sanitation and safe drinking water leading to spread of communicable diseases like cholera and diarrhoea, especially among children.

Of the many ills of rapid urbanization is the growing problem of violence, drugs and crime. Slums are a breeding ground for criminals which are readily exploited by anti-social and anti-national elements in the underworld for nefarious activities. As a result, maintaining law and order in these unplanned sprawling slums often becomes a headache for law enforcing agencies.

My father would often say, "India is not a Dharamsala that anybody could walk in—why, what for? We have our own priorities and issues". True. India has its own set of problems and priorities biggest of them being internal and external security against terrorism. India cannot let anybody walk in and settle all over its territory. Even from humanitarian point of view, the government's priority is the safety and security of Indian citizens.

5.5 Environmental Degradation

The problem of environmental degradation is a major crisis before the world. Various national and international efforts to allay the problem and mitigate the situation have so far yielded little. Its enormity is squarely attributed to two factors namely the unrelenting quest for economic growth and demographic explosion.

Industrialization: It is generally seen that poverty and

population pressures in developing economies force people to cultivate even more marginal lands. This further erodes the thin soil and depletes shallow water resources thereby creating even greater poverty, as crop yields fall and women spend even more hours each day collecting firewood and fodder and fetching water. This furious pace of economic growth through rapid industrialization has resulted in ruthless exploitation of earth's natural resources and precipitated the ecological crisis.

From the closing decades of the 18th century beginning with England, the rapid pace of industrialization led economic growth, fuelled by cheap fossil fuel, led to tremendous increase in the exploitation of natural resources. This resulted in the total value of goods and services in the market to touch the two trillion dollars mark in 1900. It jumped to 5.37 trillion in 1950 and to 30 trillion in the year 2000. At the same time, use of energy increased by almost sixteen times during the century. During the same period, carbon-dioxide emissions also increased fifteen-fold.

"Industrialization had great attraction because it could provide to the masses things for consumption and, to the affluent, still higher living standard. It could bring profits to firms engaged in industry, mining or electricity generation. To the state, politicians, and bureaucrats, it could provide prestige and political power. In short, the quest for economic growth became the mantra of the twentieth century—the creed of not only capitalists, but also communists and nationalists". [11]

"Policy makers in the communist countries, like policy makers in the developed world, were also motivated by quest for economic development and state power. Marx and Engels had shown enthusiasm for conquering nature and believed that nature exists to be harnessed by labour. After the communist state emerged in Russia, technological capability, ideological zeal, and political ambition made Soviet officials, scientists and engineers undertake gigantic projects in the name of the people. Stalin adopted the Five Year Plans with a view to industrializing his country with extraordinary speed. Energy guzzling and pollution producing industries—steel, ships and chemicals—were encouraged. After 1948, Moscow led industrialization spread to all countries east of the Iron Curtain as well as to Siberia. During the Cold War period, the United States and the Soviet Union were locked in an economic, military and public relations struggle, for which the construction of dams and other projects, both within their countries and outside, became symbols of power. The environmental aspect of this politico-economic activity did not enter their calculations.

During the first half of the 20th century, energy use and technological change made a fainter impact. The economy of the entire colonized world was controlled by the colonial powers who wanted to maximize the extraction of resources for their own benefit. They also used cheap labour and resources of their colonies to execute large-scale public works. This eventually led to the depletion of resources and damage to the ecosystem through deforestation, soil erosion and desertification whose impact is being felt now.

Population Boom: Likewise, the 20th century witnessed a four-fold increase in the world's population from 1.65 billion in 1900 to 6.6 billion in 2002. The staggering population growth in Africa and Asia changed the demographic balance with the majority of world's poor concentrated in these two continents. While the number of poor is steadily going up and is likely to reach 1.5 billion by 2025, the world population is likely to touch the 9.7 billion mark by 2050.

This steady unbridled rise in world population is an important factor in unprecedented increase in food demand, water scarcity, deforestation and air pollution leading to unmanageable climate change and natural disasters with the potential to quickly undermine all progress in human development. Climate change, in particular, has emerged as a huge challenge for the entire mankind as it jeopardizes lives and livelihoods of poor and marginalized people through food insecurity, health and other attendant risks. Therefore, this uncontrolled demographic explosion has created a general feeling that this 'population bomb' poses the severest threat to the ecosystem and that increase in population defeats the very purpose of development. [12]

Therefore, the most obvious solution to this impending ecological disaster is to control the culture of growth in population, consumption of non-renewable energy resources and air and water pollution. Or else, await the doomsday!

5.6 Corruption

Corruption, like water, flows from higher level to the lower level. Corruption at high places has a ripple effect on the entire socio-economic-political fabric of a given milieu. What might have started in the backlog of history as an expensive 'nazraana' to the superior to curry favours or a petty 'bakshish' to the subordinate for small errands, corruption today is not just a practice but a well-entrenched institution in itself. All pervasive corruption eats into the vitals of any nation. From 'kick-backs' in official deals to the so called 'commissions' for party funds, the wide range and depth of corrupt practices have overthrown governments the world over from Japan to India and the Philippines.

The magnitude of corruption at high places in the erstwhile Eastern Bloc countries revealed after the fall of the Iron Curtain and the disintegration of the Soviet Union was an eye-opener for the entire world. Likewise, stories about corrupt party functionaries within the highly regimented authoritarian structure in communist China and North Korea are equally well-known.

Today corruption, defined as the use of one's position for illegitimate private gains, has become endemic to human nature. It is a sheer waste of precious time and money that could be utilized elsewhere for public good. It is a serious problem in countries where governments and bureaucracy lack transparency in functioning. The menace of corruption is widespread in the developing world where corrupt politicians and bureaucrats tend to make huge fortunes for themselves and

On the other hand, the number of terror attacks in Pakistan reduced by 27 percent to 734 in 2016 from 1,010 in 2015.

However, a crucial difference needs to be noted while comparing India and Pakistan vis-à-vis the incidence of terror. Pakistan is largely a victim of its home-grown terror outfits that it has harboured and raised since the Soviet occupation of Afghanistan. Its extremist seminaries or madrassas, run by the likes of Hafiz Sayeed, attract terror recruits from around the world including Uighur separatists from China's Xinjiang, and the Rohingyas from Myanmar. India, on the other hand, has to deal with terror groups operating from safe havens in Pakistan. In fact, Pakistan is waging a proxy war on India through these terror attacks.

Besides Pakistani terror groups, the US analysis has labelled Naxals as the third most deadly terror organization in the world after the IS and Taliban, even ahead of Boko Haram. The CPI (Maoist) was behind 336 terror attacks last year in which 174 people were killed and 141 were injured. More than half of the terror attacks in India in 2016 took place in states such as Jammu and Kashmir, Chattisgarh, Manipur and Jharkhand. The geographical areas show that left wing extremism led by Maoists also contributed to terror incidents in parts of East India.

According to the study, the worst victim of terrorism was Jammu and Kashmir that saw an upsurge of 93 percent in terror attacks in 2016, the study says. The Indian Ministry of Home Affairs, however, reports a 54.81 percent increase in terror incidents in the state. However, the good thing is that the Government of India has taken a tough line against terrorism. It has decided not to seek a political outreach and concentrate on intensive security operations, going by the assessment that negotiations only signal weakness rather than accommodation, it says.

As per the NCSTRT data, the total number of people kidnapped or taken hostage in terrorist attacks in India has, however, reduced from 866 in 2015 to 317 in 2016. On an average, terrorist attacks in India caused 0.4 deaths per attack in 2016, compared to 2.4 deaths per attack worldwide. Nearly three quarters of attacks i.e. 73 percent in India in 2016 were non-lethal.

The deadliest terror attack in India took place in July 2016 when Naxals attacked CRPF men in Bihar in which 16 people, including assailants, were killed. The US report says that nearly two-third of terrorist attacks in India were carried out by Naxals as compared to other countries that experienced most terror attacks in 2016, the diversity of perpetrator groups was much larger in India, with 52 active groups. There were 45 terror groups listed by the US in its 2015 report. The US had identified 334 groups and organizations behind terror attacks in 2016 worldwide, while there were 288 such groups active in 2015.

It says that the number of total attacks worldwide in 2016 were reduced by nine percent to 11,072 against 12,121 in 2015 and total deaths worldwide also reduced by 13 percent in 2016 to 25,621 as compared to 2015 that reported 29,424 fatalities. This was largely due to fewer attacks and deaths in Afghanistan, Syria, Nigeria, Pakistan and Yemen, it said. Around 55 percent of all attacks took place in Iraq, Afghanistan, India, Pakistan and the Philippines out of 104 terror affected countries, while 75 percent of all deaths due to terror occurred in Iraq, Afghanistan, Syria, Nigeria and Pakistan.

5.9 Internal Security

There can be no lasting peace and development without internal security. In the absence of internal security, everything goes waste be it money, labour, time or energy. Thus, when it comes to safety and security of the common man in the street, who is the end user of all developmental initiatives, nothing else matters. What ultimately counts is the safety and security of the ordinary citizens, peace at borders and hassle free passage within the country without any sabotage like engineered road and rail accidents through punctured tyres and fiddled nuts and bolts. It is, therefore, high-time to understand that it is not development alone but internal security that ought to be the top priority.

In fact, development is meaningless without peace and internal security. The menace of Maoist inspired naxalism, for instance, is the main impediment on the road to development in naxal-affected states that constitute the heartland of India. And, it would not be wished away by either hugging the deceptive Chinese or trading in their substandard goods and services. Public appeals for the boycott of Chinese goods particularly on festive occasions like Rakhabandhan and Deepawali serve no purpose when the governments, both state and central, do not hesitate in signing huge deals with the Chinese companies that specialize in spy ware even in mobile telephony and act as sappers and miners for the PRC. Clearly, one cannot run with the hare and hunt with the hound.

Likewise, youngsters in the Kashmir valley, who willingly neglect their studies to pelt stones at security forces, idolize traitors like terrorists Burhan Wani and aspire to follow in his footsteps, can neither appreciate nor value development. While they indulge in anti-national activities, their vociferous and belligerent supporters justify them on grounds of underdevelolpment and lack of education and employment opportunities in the state. But they conveniently forget the truth that those, who burn down schools and colleges, hardly care for education and employment. In fact, money is not the issue here. They get enough of it from their terrorist handlers in Pakistan. This was revealed during the recent NIA raids on the over ground Kashmiri separatist leaders, who are hand in glove with the jihadists of Pakistan and the IS. Therefore, education and employment are hollow words as far as the separatists in terrorist-infested states like Jammu and Kashmir are concerned.

As regards the people in the valley, if they had really wanted their children to study well in safe and peaceful environs, they would not have raised a bogey of separatism against India and learnt something from the plight of their fellow bretheren in Pak-occupied Kashmir (POK).

As such education and career have little importance for a terrorist. Experience has shown that under the influence of Islamist radicalism spread by the likes of Zakir Naik even highly qualified men and women like engineers and doctors from India's southern states rush to join the ISIS network both within and outside the country. These anti-social and anti-national elements are now using coaching institutions to catch vulnerable youth to radicalize them. What is worse, those who convert young girls from other faiths into Islam are handsomely rewarded as an incentive. The situation in Western Uttar Pradesh, Assam and West Bengal bordering Bangladesh is no different where heavy infestation of anti-social and anti-national radicalized elements is a harsh reality. The growing influence of SIMI (the Students Islamic Movement of India) and the PFI (the Popular Front of India) in Kerala proves the point.

Therefore, what India urgently needs is a strong civil defence mechanism to ease the pressure on already overburdened military and para-military forces and a wide network of broad strategic roads and bridges across the country for smooth and speedy transportation of armed forces and equipment to international borders with China, Pakistan and Bangladesh. For instance, the reality of infrastructure development in Jammu and Kashmir is exposed by the sorry state of narrow roads such as the one linking Jammu to strategically located Akhnoor, famous for the coronation of Maharaja Ranjeet Singh on the banks of river Chenab. This situation needs to be corrected at the earliest.

Since India is consistently a victim of relentless proxy war and terrorism from jihadist Pakistan, no Indian can afford to lower his or her guard against Islamist or naxalite terrorism. This is particularly so after the Amarnath Yatra terror attack, in which a bus carrying pilgrims from Gujarat was attacked in which eight people were killed and 19 injured. The terrorists this time adopted an altogether different modus operandi. They first isolated the bus from the caravan on the pretext of showing Srinagar to the pilgrims and then engineered a puncture that took hours and hours to get repaired. They took advantage of the situation by spraying bullets on the stranded passengers. One wonders, why in the first place, the gullible tourists allowed themselves to be befooled on the pretext of visiting volatile Srinagar; secondly, why the bus operator did not keep more spare wheels, more than normally required, to meet any exigency in a troubled state like Jammu and Kashmir; and, thirdly, why it never occurred to them as to why the punctured tyre was taking so long to get repaired?

This incident has a lesson for every patriotic Indian and that is: if the Kashmir valley was really as safe and secure as a heaven on earth then the native Kashmiri Hindus, displaced in millions, would have been living there since long. They would not have been thrown out of their native land by their own kith and kin who got converted to Islam by the sword. Then the schools and other educational institutions, like the skill development centre, so vital for development in the state, would not have been burnt down. And, those who appeared so friendly and helpful to the victims of Amarnath terror attack, would not have been raising the banner of secession and giving arms training to their women and children to make their secessionist activities look like indigenous struggle for independence on the lines of Palestinian uprising or intifada.

5.10 Future Challenges

Sometimes governments have to take hard decisions and ensure strict tasking to move people out of their long lethargic slumber. But care should be taken to see that these hard decisions do not inconvenience the people too much. To minimize the impact of hard economic and fiscal reforms, affirmative administrative reforms must first be put in place. At the same time, the government should ensure the continuation of certain best practices of the past. In all this, the principle of parity must be observed at all cost. The government must not discriminate between one citizen and the other on the basis of caste, creed or religion.

As regards economic policy, the government should see that it remains progress-oriented and not control-oriented. The State should be free to monitor and to some extent regulate it, but it should not try to control it. There should be some space for loose ends which could help a nation survive in times of distress. More importantly, doubts about the effectiveness of demonetization and appropriateness of the implementation of the goods and services tax or GST should not be allowed to cast shadow on a government which earnestly devotes itself to the cause of development.

Today, India ranks 131 among the 188 countries on the human development index (HDI) score while Norway is number one at 0.949, Australia and Switzerland share the score at 0.939. The HDI is a measure for assessing progress in three basic dimensions of human development: a long and healthy life, access to knowledge, and access to decent standard of living.

According to the 2016 Human Development Report (HDR), India's HDI value of 0.624 puts it in the 'medium human development' category, alongside countries such as Congo, Namibia and Pakistan. It is ranked third among the SAARC countries, behind Sri Lanka (73) and the Maldives (105), both of which figure in the 'high human development' category.

While India's HDI value increased from 0.428 in 1990 to 0.624 in 2015, it still had the lowest rank among BRICS nations. However, its average annual growth in HDI (1990-2015) was higher than that of other medium HD countries.

The report says about 1.5 billion people worldwide still live in multidimensional poverty, 54 percent of them concentrated in South Asia alone. While poverty fell significantly from 1990 to 2015, inequalities sharpened in the region. For instance, India's HDI score fell by 27 percent due to regional disparities in education, health and living standards within the country.

South Asia also had the highest levels of malnutrition in the world, at 38 percent, and the lowest public health expenditure as a percentage of the GDP. India's public health expenditure was even lower at 1.4 percent of the GDP. However, it did make some gains between 1990 and 2015, improving life expectancy by 10.4 years in this period. Child malnutrition also declined by 10 percentage points from 2015 as there was a modest gain in infant and under-five mortality rates.

The report also hailed the national rural employment guarantee scheme as a 'prime example' of 'combining social protection with appropriate employment strategies'. "The success of national development programmes like Skill India, Digital India, Make in India and Beti Bacho Beti Padhao, aimed at bridging gaps in human development, will be crucial in ensuring the success of "Agenda 2030", said Uri Afanasiev, the UN resident coordinator for India, while referring to the Sustainable Development Goals. "These programmes, and the long-running affirmative action measure, illustrate the government's commitment to identifying and mapping human development deficits, as well as taking action to achieve the SFGs", he said.

Clearly, India's road to peace and prosperity through sustainable development is full of challenges such as terrorism and demographic explosion that not only undo all the progress but also threaten the future of humanity. As a result, the whole world is trying to put up a unified fight against the menace of terrorism perpetrated by the axis of evil. In these tumultuous times, the famous words by the US President Thomas Jefferson: "Eternal vigilance is the price of liberty" should be the guiding light of every peace-loving global citizens, particularly Indians facing incessant terrorism from Pakistan.

Certainly, India can meet these challenges head on. This requires a clear understanding of the imminent threats and paying close attention to issues and concerns at hand such as:

1. Development: Development is a chain process. If one

region develops, the adjoining region also develops. It gives impetus for development to all the regions which are economically connected with the adjoining region. Similarly, lack of development in one region would promote underdevelopment or slow down the pace of development in the adjoining region as well. This should be kept in mind during developmental planning.

2. Development should be balanced and all around. It should be evenly executed. No particular sector should be overdeveloped at the cost and neglect of the other. High cost projects with long gestation period should be avoided while low cost smaller projects for rural development should be promoted to instil a sense of relief among the masses.
3. Terrorism is a huge obstacle in the way of development not because it slows downs the pace by derailing it, but because it destroys the agents of change: People who are involved in bringing about development along with infrastructure and other wherewithal are lost due to terrorist activities. This creates terror in the minds of those people who are going to benefit most from the development. Terrorism prevents participation, adds to the cost of development and minimizes the human and material benefits accruing from it.
4. Terrorism reduces the scope, the magnitude and the beneficial impact of development everywhere. Therefore, if the world has to benefit from various developmental objectives laid down in the Agenda 2030 for Sustainable Development, then terrorism must be banished from the face of the earth. Terrorism impedes development. Development, if not allowed, could cause socio-economic inequalities like the income and gender inequality and regional disparities like the rural-urban divide. This goes against the principle of parity.
5. Terrorism and development are inversely proportional. The tenets of terrorism are against humanity. Terrorists want more

and more people to be involved in terrorist activities. The people and communities who lose lives through terrorism are at a demographic loss. Population growth in the terrorists and terrorism-supporting communities and peace-loving, terrorism-victim communities is diametrically opposite. If this trend continues, then the benefit of development that has already taken place will accrue to these terrorists and terrorism-supporting communities and not peace-loving terrorism-victim communities.

6. Therefore, it is the responsibility of not one nation, but the entire comity of nations working under the auspices of the United Nations to stop terrorism at all costs. Even if it implies annihilating the terrorist and terrorism supporting communities and the nation states whose political masters support terrorism in the larger good of humanity and development. Violence against one to establish peace in the rest of the world is quite justifiable.

Endnotes

1. Hobsbawm, Eric (1994), "Age of Extremes: The Short Twentieth Century (1914-1991)", London; Abacus.
2. Ibid.
3. Human Development Report, 2016.
4. Ministry of Home Affairs, Government of India. The data is up to June 9, 2017.
5. Ibid.
6. UNDP Report, 1991.
7. UNDP Report, 2016
8. Ibid.
9. Ibid.
10. Ibid.
11. Mahajan, Sneh (2010), "Issues in Twentieth-Century World History", New Delhi: Macmillan.
12. Ehrlich, P.R. (1972), "The Population Bomb", New York: Valentine Books.
13. Madhok, Balraj (n.d.), "Nationalism, Democracy and Social Change", New Delhi: Deepak Prakashan
14. Ibid.

15. Madhok, Balraj (1978), "Reflections of a Detenu", New Delhi: Newman Publishers.
16. Ibid.
17. Madhok, Balraj (1978), 'Reflections of a Detenu', New Delhi: Newman Publishers.

Bibliography

Bibliography

A. Primary Sources:
Reports, Documents and Articles

Aggarwal, Aradhana (2002), "Anti-dumping Law and Practice: An Indian Perspective", ICREAR.

Constitution of India.

Brandt Commission Report, 1981.

Economic Survey, 2016-17.

"Maitland Commission: The Missing Link", Report of the International Commission for Worldwide Telecommunications Development, 1989.

Sen, Amartya (2000), "How to Judge Globalism?", *The American Prospects*, 13, 1, January 1-14.

UNDP (1991), Human Development Report, 1991.

UNDP (1993), Human Development Report, 1993.

UNDP (2002), Human Development Report, 2002.

UNDP (2013), Human Development Report, 2013.

UNDP (2015), Human Development Report, 2015.

UNDP (2016), Human Development Report, 2016.

UNESCO (1977), World Communication Report, 1977.

UNESCO (1982), The MacBride Commission Report, 1982.

UNRISD (2016), Policy Innovations for Transformative Change, 2016.

US State Department Report (2016), National Consortium for the Study of Terrorism and Response to Terrorism, 2016.

World Bank (1973), World Development Report, 1973.

World Bank (2014), World Development Report, 2014.

World Commission on Environment and Development Report, 1987.

World Congress of Communication for Development Report, 2006.

B. Secondary Sources:

Adelman, I. and C.T. Morris (1973), "Economic Growth and Social Equity in Developing Countries", California: Stanford University Press.

Ariyaratne, A.T. (1987), "Beyond Development Communication: Case Study on Sarvodaya, Sri Lanka", in N. Jayaweera and S. Amunugama (eds.), 'Rethinking Development Communication',

Singapore: Asian Mass Communication Research and Information Centre.

Ascroft, Joseph and Sipho Masilela (1989), "From Top-Down to Co-Equal Communication: Popular Participation in Development Decision-Making", paper presented at the seminar on Participation: A Key Concept in Communication and Change, University of Poona, India.

Dagron, Alfonso G. (2001), "Making Waves: Stories of Participatory Communication for Social Change", New York: The Rockfeller Foundation.

Dreze Jean and A. Sen (2005), "India: Development and Participation", New Delhi: Oxford University Press.

Dissanayake, W. (1984), "A Buddhist Approach to Development: A Sri Lankan Endeavour", in G. Wang and W. Dissanayake (eds.), 'Continuity and Change in Communication Systems', New Jersey: Ablex.

Dunn, P.D. (1978), "Appropriate Technology", New York: Schocken Books.

Dutt, Romesh (1960), "The Economic History of India: Under Early British Rule (1757-1873)", Vol. I. Government of India, Ministry of Information and Broadcasting, New Delhi.

Fyes, Fred (1976), "Communication and Development", unpublished Paper, College of Communications, University of Illinois: Urbana-Champaign.

Goulet, D. (1971), "The Cruel Choice: A New Concept in Theory of Development", New York: Atheneum.

Gunder Frank, A. (1969), "Capitalism and Underdevelopment in Latin America", New York: Monthly Review Press.

Hamelink, L. (1979), "Informatics: Third World Call for New Order", *Journal for Communications*, 29.

Hedebro, Goran (1982), "Communication and Social Change in Developing Nations: A Critical View", Ames: Iowa State University Press.

Hobsbawm, Eric (1995), "Age of Extremes: The Short Twentieth Century (1914-1991)", London: Abacus.

Hornik, Robert (1988), "Development Communication: Information, Agriculture and Nutrition in the Third World", New York: Longman.

Inkeles, Alex (1969), "Making Men Modern: On the Causes and Consequences of Individual Change in Six Countries', *American*

Journal of Sociology, 75, September.

Kapila, Uma (2015), "Indian Economy: Performance and Policies", New Delhi: Academic Foundation.

Katz, Elihu and P. Lazarsfeld (1955), "Personal Influence", New York: Free Press.

Katz, Elihu (1963), "The Diffusion of New Ideas and Practices", in Wilbur Schramm (ed.), 'The Science of Human Communication', New York: Basic Books.

Kindelberger, C.P. (1965), "Economic Development".

Kumar, Keval J. (1994), "Mass Communication in India", Bombay: Jaico Publications.

Kronenburg, J. (1986), "Empowerment of the Poor: A Comparative Analysis of Two Development Endeavours in Kenya", cited in Jan Servaes.

Lasswell, Harold (1948), "The Structure and Function of Communication in Society", in Lyman Bryson (ed.), 'The Communication of Ideas', New York: Harper and Brothers.

Lazarsfeld, P., and H. Band Gaudet (1998), "The People's Choice", New York: Colombia Press.

Lerner, D. (1958), "The Passing of Traditional Society", New York: Free Press.

Lewis, Arthur W. (1963), "Is Economic Growth Desirable?", in Allen and Unwin (eds.), 'Theory of Economic Growth', London: Harper.

Madhok, Balraj (n.d.), "Nationalism, Democracy and Social Change", Delhi: Deepak Prakashan.

Madhok, Balraj (1978), "Reflections of a Detenue", New Delhi: Newman Publishers.

Mahajan, Sneh (2010), "Issues in Twentieth-Century World History", New Delhi: MacMillan.

Mankiw, Gregory N. (2012), "Principles of Economics", Cengage Learning.

Masmoudi, M. (1979), "The New World Information Order", *Journal of Communication*, 29, 2.

McQuail, D. (1994), "Mass Communication Theory: An Introduction", London: Sage Publications.

Melkote, Srinivas R. (1991), "Communication for Development in the Third World: Theory and Practice", New Delhi: Sage Publications.

Myrdal, Gunnar (1970), "The Challenge of World Poverty", New

York: Vintage Books.

Nordenstreng, K. (1986), "New Information Communication Order Source Book", Prague: International Organisation for Journalists.

Oshima, Harry T. (1976), "Development and Mass Communication: A Re-Examination" in W. Shramm and D. Lerner (eds.), 'Communication and Change', Honolulu: University of Hawaii.

Rogers, Everett M. (1962), "Diffusion of Innovations", New York: Free Press.

Rogers, Everett M. (1962), "Diffusion of Innovations", New York: The Free Press.

Rogers, Everett M. (1976), "The Passing of Dominant Paradigm: Reflections on Diffusion Research", in W. Shramm and D. Lerner (eds.), 'Communication and Change', Honolulu: University Press of Hawaii.

Schramm, W. (1964), "Mass Media and National Development: The Role of Information in the Developing Countries", Stanford, CA: Stanford University Press.

Schumacher, E.F. (1973), "Small is Beautiful", New York: Harper and Row.

Seers, Dudley (1977), "The Meaning of Development", *International Development Review,* XIX (2).

Sen, Amartya (2000), "Development as Freedom", New Delhi: Oxford University Press.

Servaes, J. (1996), "Media and Development: Alternative Perspectives", Leicester, UK: Centre for Mass Communication Research, University of Leicester.

Singhal, Arvind and Everett M. Rogers (2001), "India's Communication Revolution: From Bullock Carts to Cyber Marts", New Delhi: Sage Publications.

Somavia, Juan (1976), "The Transnational Power Structure and International Information", *Development Dialogue*, 2.

Stiglitz, Joseph (2002), "Globalization and its Discontents", New Delhi: Penguin.

Streeten, Paul (1979), "Development Ideas in Historic Perspective", in Kim Q. Hill (ed.), 'Towards a New Strategy for Development', New York: Pergamon Press.

Tardm, Gabriel (1930), "The Laws of Imitation", New York: Holt.

Thussu, Daya Kishan (ed.) (2010), "International Communication: A Reader", London: Routledge.

Todaro, M. (2008), "Economic Development", New Delhi: Pearson.

Uphoff, Norman and M. Esman (1974), "Local Organisation for Rural Development: Analysis of Asian Experience", New York: Centre for International Studies, Cornell University.

Wang, Georgette and Wimal Dissanayake (1984), "Culture, Development and Change: Some Explorative Observations", in G. Wang and W. Dissanayake (eds.), 'Continuity and Change in Communication Systems', New Jersey: Ablex.

Weaver, James H. and Kenneth Jameson (1978), "Economic Development: Competing Paradigms, Competing Parables", Washington D.C.: Development Studies Programme, Agency for International Development.

Williams, Kevin (2003), "Understanding Media Theory", London: Arnold.

Index

Index